ONCE UPON A TIME IN WIGAN

ONCE UPON A TIME IN WIGAN

by Mick Martin

JOSEF WEINBERGER PLAYS

LONDON

ONCE UPON A TIME IN WIGAN
First published in 2003
by Josef Weinberger Ltd
12-14 Mortimer Street, London, W1T 3JJ

ISBN 0 85676 271 7

To northern soul lovers everywhere –
past, present and future!

ONCE UPON A TIME IN WIGAN was first produced by Urban Expansions at the Contact Theatre, Manchester, on 18 February 2003, in associaton with the Contact Theatre and West Yorkshire Playhouse. The cast was as follows:

EUGENE	Richard Oldham
MAXINE	Sally Carman
DANNY	Steven Hillman
SUZANNE	Christine Roberts

Directed by Paul Sadot

Designed by Giuseppe Belli and Emma Barrington-Binns

Lighting Designed by David Martin

The production subsequently transferred to the Quarry Theatre, West Yorkshire Playhouse, Leeds on 11 March 2003.

AUTHOR'S NOTE

The original Urban Expansions production of this play used a great deal of video and slide imagery to convey not only the magic of Wigan Casino (original footage of the Casino was used) but also a sense of the times in which the play is set, the late 70s, early 80s. On a couple of occasions the screens also served to actually move the story on, for example the early happy days of Eugene's and Maxine's love affair, where the story perforce jumps on time-wise. Whilst it worked well and enhanced the production, it is not entirely necessary to the play and the lack of it ought not deter future productions.

At the end of the script printed here you will find a list of credits, almost like a post script, and these were projected onto the screens. Again they are not absolutely necessary, and could be spoken in voice over. I felt it appropriate to give some sense of 'where they are now' to the characters, and also to mention and credit Russ Winstanley by name – after all, he it was who founded the club and gave everyone so much pleasure. His assistance and support to the director, Paul Sadot, and myself in the original production was absolutely invaluable.

Obviously the musical content of the piece is paramount, but a track listing seems superfluous, and any future director may well have their own personal play list of tunes that he or she feel best capture the moments and nuances of the play. Suffice it to say that music featured extensively, often underscoring the scenes but equally often taking centre stage itself as the characters danced and enjoyed the experiences of Wigan Casino. That said, at the time of writing there is a CD due for production in tandem with the show so a copy of that will give a clear indication of which tracks were used. Obviously the '3 before 8' choose themselves, as does Frank Wilson's 'Do I Love You', the very last tune ever played at the Casino.

It was and still is beautiful music, the dance style that grew on the floor at Wigan and a few other all-nighters, all sited in the declining industrial towns in the north, is a spectacle to behold in itself. The whole scene had a wonderful quality of being almost secret, dark, magical. And yet for all that northern soul is if anything bigger today than it was back in the 70s, and that is because the music is timeless. That the majority of northern classics never had commercial success upon their initial release has partly helped that, of course. Somewhere along the line this obscure black music, American tunes from the 60s and 70s, struck a chord with kids in the industrial working class north of England, the scene revitalized the careers of artists who thought their time had been and gone, how wonderful it must have been for them to discover that whilst they were a car park attendant in Philadelphia, Pittsburgh or wherever, they were a hero in Wigan! They came from Scotland, Wales, Cornwall, all across the globe actually, to hear the music and dance to it, but the north of England was the heartland, and it still is.

Long may it continue, it will do, no doubt about that.

Mick Martin
March 2003

ACT ONE

All four actors are in the space, EUGENE *is to the forestage.
'Breakaway', the opening theme tune is playing.* EUGENE
simply listens and contemplates, DANNY, MAXINE *and* SUZANNE
commence dancing to it in their own worlds. As it ends EUGENE
commences his story.

EUGENE   Did it really . . . really happen?
            Wigan Casino . . . the former Empress Ballroom,
            1973 to 1981.

            (DANNY *enters, approaches him.* MAXINE *is
            looking intently at him now,* SUZANNE *the same.*
            EUGENE *is distant, lost in memory.*)

DANNY   Ah well . . . one last and final time brother . . .
            smile, for fuck's sake Eugene, it's just a club
            shutting down, not a funeral. Are we sorted out
            like?

EUGENE   Eh? Yeah.

DANNY   Smashing, what do I owe you?

EUGENE   What do I owe you?

DANNY   I'm not with you.

EUGENE   Danny . . . everything . . . everything good,
            everything that I remember, that ever happened to
            me . . . happened here, with you . . . with all of
            you.

DANNY   Ah well . . . you're a sad bastard, I've always said
            it.

            (DANNY *leaves* EUGENE *alone on the forestage, he
            thinks a moment.*)

EUGENE   No I'm fucking not, mate.

(*Then suddenly he looks up, directly at the
audience. He jumps to his feet and commences
telling us the story.*)

Picture this . . . a day in December, no don't, that's
Blondie, I secretly quite liked Blondie and bought
a couple of their albums by the way, don't tell
anyone. No, picture this . . .

Me and my mate Lee, he were from Bolton as well,
haven't seen him in years, you'll get why later, but
I owe him my life.
He comes round one night with a tape . . .
'Here Eugene . . . stick this on!'
What is it?
'It's a tape.'
I can see it's a fuckin tape Lee, but what's on it?
'Put it on, our kid gave it to me . . . it's
unbelievable . . .'

(*The tape kicks in, all four have their first
experience of listening to the music, we watch
them enter a higher plain, a most spiritual
experience overtakes them.*)

Northern soul music? Northern soul . . . Fuck me,
what a belting name!
Where is it? Where do they play it? How can you
buy it!? How do we get there . . . ?
Picture it . . . 18 years old . . . a butcher in Bolton
meat market . . . a dickhead on the piss every
Friday, Saturday, and Sunday, till the money ran
out basically . . . well, no more!

Wigan Casino . . . a paradise, an oasis, bubbling
with amphetamine, in a world so drab they should
have called it off.

(*He builds himself up in terms of adrenalin and
enthusiasm through the following.*)

1976, my first time . . . we bought tickets . . . I gave
Lee the money for my ticket . . . Lee went to get
the tickets . . . we had the tickets!

We got up to the door, fuck me what a queue,
massive scrum, but so what 'cos we had tickets!
And the bouncer took one look at us tickets and
said,
'Sorry lads forgeries! Come back another time.'
'Forgeries', I said? 'Forgeries! Fucking forgeries!
Lee!?'
Picture this, two idiots like demented terrier
fucking dogs out the back of Wigan Casino, in the
pissing down!
Point being we'd scored a load of speed in the
café round the back and quaffed the lot in gleeful
anticipation!
Wigan bastard Casino!

(*He sits down, puts his head in hands, rolls,
groans in anguish.*)

The worst night of my entire fucking life!
And I've had some shit ones, believe you me!
And then . . . she came to me . . . an angel . . . in a
puddle.

(MAXINE *enters, she looks at him a moment. He is
speechless to begin with, she is bathed in a nice
white light.* MAXINE *is outside to cool down. This
is the first time she and* EUGENE *meet. A most
beautifully romantic tune plays.*)

MAXINE   (*cutting across the music*) What you sat out here
for, dick'ead?

(*He is too awestruck to speak, or too freaked out
by the speed he's just done.*)

It's fantastic in there!

EUGENE   Is it?

MAXINE   Yeah . . . are you alright mate, you look a bit . . .
fucked up.

EUGENE   Do I? I . . . I am . . . I'm fucked up . . . utterly . . .
who are you?

MAXINE   Why don't you go inside then, it's ace!

EUGENE   Is that why you're out here then?

MAXINE   Just come for some fresh air, you got any fags?
            What you doing?

EUGENE   Eh? Oh I love a freezing cold February night . . .
            sat outside in the slashing it down.

            (*He fishes out a fag for her.*)

MAXINE   Be a funny get then.

EUGENE   I wish I could be. I've come all the way here, I've
            no way of getting home, my ticket's a forgery and
            add to that my lifelong mate Lee's a complete
            knobhead.

MAXINE   I see. Where is he?

EUGENE   He's gone for a run.

MAXINE   At this time?

EUGENE   He isn't thinking about the time.

MAXINE   Oh well . . . have you not been here before?

EUGENE   No. You?

MAXINE   First time . . . I hate discos normally . . . this is
            brilliant though . . . no tossy DJs, fancy lighting
            . . . and the dancing! Man, some o' them lads in
            there are . . . it!

EUGENE   Thanks . . . you're not making it any easier.

MAXINE   Sorry. You a good dancer?

EUGENE   The best.

MAXINE   Oh aye . . . show us then.

EUGENE   Out here? In the freezing cold? My joints have
           seized up.

MAXINE   I'll believe you . . . thousands wouldn't. Give us
           your hand.

EUGENE   What do you want with my hand?

           (*She fishes in her pocket, produces a black
           eyeliner, makes a smudge mark on his hand, the
           same as the one on hers.*)

EUGENE   What's that gonna do?

MAXINE   You can come back in with me now, can't you?

EUGENE   Can I?

MAXINE   I'll allow you . . . just this once mind . . . you're on
           your own then. Just show it to the bouncer as you
           pass him, dead cool, he'll have no idea.

EUGENE   Dead cool, you say . . . I think I see what you
           mean. I'm Eugene.

MAXINE   I don't mind who you are.

EUGENE   Do you not. Who are you?

MAXINE   Ah . . .

EUGENE   Well, thank you very much 'Ah' . . . you're very
           kind.

MAXINE   It's perfectly alright.

EUGENE   What's your name?

MAXINE   Like I said, dead cool . . .

           (*A suitable tune for the moment/experience of
           love at first sight* EUGENE *has just had. She leads
           him into the Casino – it is magical. A swirl of*

> *moving images proliferate around screens and*
> *projection surfaces, perhaps in slow motion.*
> EUGENE *is awestruck. Suddenly the track changes*
> *to an upbeat stomping number, the lights come up*
> *full, swinging round and round the place as*
> EUGENE *comes out of his trance and takes it all in.*
> DANNY *and* SUZANNE *are out on the dance floor*
> *going for it with* MAXINE. *This sequence should be*
> *a full-throttle visually/aurally exhilerating*
> *sweep, the full impact of entering Wigan Casino*
> *for the first time.)*

EUGENE   Oh, man alive! I stood gazing, awestruck, at the
            pure rhythmic splendour of that dance floor . . .
            alright, just her then . . . really . . . something . . .
            but more than her, the music, the disaster waiting
            to get in . . . what I truly deep down remember . . .
            was the heat, like a furnace door opening . . .

            And the fuckin' smell! Jesus Christ! Sweat!

            Phet sweat, vinegar sweat, armpit sweat!
            Sweat running down your face,
            Cloggin' up your eyes, sweat sticking to you
            Like   . . . like sweat, wet and clammy dirty brown
            cigarette sweat, rising like an ocean of sweat, a full
            weight mega-tsunami of sweat!
            Black sweat and white getting together to form an
            unbelievably rich and harmonious multi-cultural
            diverse and thereby fascinating hybrid brand of
            sweat such as never was sweated before!
            And here's me in the middle of it all, aye man,
            Sound, how you doin'? Good to see you! Crackin',
            couldn't be better!
            Falling off the ceiling in yellow brown drops
            And landing on your lovely clean top sweat,
            Like a great big cauldron of sweat and you can
            swim in it. And man, did I!
            For hours . . . and hours . . . and beautiful lovely
            hours!

            (*At this point he breaks off and joins in the*
            dancing. Alas, the lad cannot actually dance and

*is speeding off his tits so he can't stop himself
blathering on as well.*)

Now the first record I ever heard through that
sticky shit sweat was Don Ray, 'Born A Loser' . . .
man that's me! If this is being a loser then please
God may I never win a fucking thing ever again!

(EUGENE *is aware that he cannot really dance,
much as he keeps trying, so at length he stops
and simply observes. Cut the track, simply*
MAXINE *dancing – perhaps she is in his mind's
eye on the screen as he speaks.*)

EUGENE   Shape, hips, rhythm, flow . . .
           She's perfect. She's doing it all for me. I could
           watch her all night.
           I am watching her all night . . . moving, all night . . .
           for me.
           I've got big plans for that girl . . . big bad plans . . .
           big fuckin great plans.
           Me and her on the great soul plain . . . like
           Hiawatha and Minnehaha . . .
           On my scooter . . . she'll look the dogs on the back
           of my scooter . . .
           Picture it . . . Hiawatha and Minnehaha on a
           scooter . . . what am I on about, fucking drugs,
           that'll be me and her, riding free . . .
           Me mate Lee'll have to walk, though . . . he'll
           understand.
           Shouldn't have cocked up getting the tickets up,
           should he?

           (*As the tune ends, applause for the DJ, and
           without thinking* EUGENE *strides straight across
           to* MAXINE.)

EUGENE   I could just lick the sweat off every inch of you!

MAXINE   (*shocked*) You what?

EUGENE   I . . . I've got sweat on every inch of . . . me . . .
           but don't worry . . . I've got to go now. Sorry.

(*He turns full-tilt away from her, runs away
screaming, head in his hands. She watches him a
moment as self-loathing/paranoia, etc, consumes
him whole. He gathers himself to take in his first
experiences of the Casino.*)

Yeah . . . that very first night in Wigan's
wonderful Casino,
I saw something . . . beautiful.
Felt something . . . other . . . deeper . . . more . . .
important . . . than my life.
Something other people didn't understand . . .
could never understand . . .
That touched me . . . like nothing else ever has.
And I didn't even know her name.

(*A tune comes in, elsewhere across the stage
DANNY is flicking through records as in the
record bar. SUZANNE is gazing dolefully at
Michael Greenhalgh.*)

DANNY   Ha!

SUZANNE   What?

DANNY   Sister Lee! Sam Ward, Detroit, 1966! I've found it!

SUZANNE   Well done.

DANNY   You don't know what this means to me!

SUZANNE   No, but . . . I'm still really happy for you.

DANNY   Oh, this is gonna make the hitch-hike home feel
             like fun . . . a treat, even.

SUZANNE   Is it really!

DANNY   Sorry . . . what's up, did you want to buy it?

SUZANNE   No . . . I'm sorry . . . Do you see that boy down
             there . . . the one in the cap sleeve T-shirt . . . with
             the nine-inch waist band . . . ?

DANNY   Aye . . . the one snogging the girl?

SUZANNE   He's called Michael Greenhalgh . . . I paid him in
             here . . . and she's my best friend! Was!

DANNY   Oh.

SUZANNE   Yeah. So enjoy Sister Lee and good luck to you!

             (SUZANNE *storms off. Cut to* EUGENE.)

EUGENE   But to get her . . . I had to do something . . . I had
             to dance like those guys could dance. And stop
             my sick mind coming out with shit like I could lick
             the sweat off you! Sick, sick, sick, fuck!

             (DANNY *resumes his dancing.* EUGENE *continues to
             be utterly entranced, mesmerized by it all. Cut to*
             SUZANNE *joining* MAXINE *in the ladies' toilet. NB:
             During the scene* EUGENE *is simply reflecting on
             the bogs in all their glory, he is not in the scene
             with them!*)

MAXINE   Urrgghh! That is disgusting . . . bloody 'ell, can't
             they afford a plumber round here?

SUZANNE   Well don't look at me, I haven't done it!

EUGENE   The bogs . . . oh the bogs, the legendary fuckin'
             bogs!

MAXINE   I aren't saying you have pet, but . . . oh, I aren't
             having a wee in here!

SUZANNE   There's not a lot of point in using the toilet, is
             there . . .

MAXINE   Place is one big toilet! Oh, I'm complaining about
             this . . . take your money off you coming in, least
             they can do is sort this out!

EUGENE   Holy bogs, sacred bogs . . . Sickening shitty bogs!

SUZANNE   My mum says it's people in Wigan generally . . .
           not the same standards.

MAXINE   As where?

SUZANNE   Us in Burnley, right people where you know
           stuff's right.

MAXINE   (*sceptical*) Right . . . I'm sure there's somat in
           that . . .

           (*Cut to* EUGENE.)

EUGENE   (*with love*) The sinking sumphole of human
           detritus
           And shite and slash and the like and wazzed out,
           Fucked up gurning phet dogs of the all night
           dance floor
           Standing, slumping, grinning, leaning . . .
           Good old Armitage Shanks, many's the hour . . .

           (*The girls are leaving the toilets now.*)

MAXINE   Are you alright?

SUZANNE   Yeah.

MAXINE   Brilliant club, in't it?

SUZANNE   Yeah.

MAXINE   I'm coming again next week, are you?

SUZANNE   Maybe . . .

MAXINE   Maybe not?

SUZANNE   No.

MAXINE   Any reason?

SUZANNE   'Cos it's the worst night of my life, I hate it, I hate
           it. I don't ever want to see this place again as long
           as I live or Michael shitty Greenhalgh lives, which

I hope is no more than the next ten minutes and
my supposed friend Carol dies in the same car
crash or landslide earthquake or whatever!

(MAXINE *is a tad freaked* – SUZANNE *betrayed
rather more anger than she intended to there.*)

MAXINE   Oh . . . So you've not enjoyed it that much at all,
           then?

SUZANNE   Oh, I didn't say that.

MAXINE   It's what it sounded like . . . who's Michael
           Greenhalgh?

SUZANNE   A right swine, you don't want to know him . . .
           tattoos, I think he steals, he wears a star jumper, I
           hate them, don't you?

MAXINE   I do, actually . . . and he was your boyfriend?

SUZANNE   No . . . but I paid him in here and he's ignored me
           all night and now he's got his tongue down my
           best mate's neck, the slut!

MAXINE   Bad.

SUZANNE   I'll kill her when I get hold of her. She's my best
           friend . . . but I hate her and I always have, truth
           be told. Does that make me bad?

MAXINE   No . . . well, yeah . . . but bad's good I've decided.
           I'm Maxine, by the way,

SUZANNE   Suzanne . . . I work at a dry cleaners in Burnley. I
           like it, dry cleaning. Two for the price of one.
           What do you do?

MAXINE   You don't want to know.

SUZANNE   I do or I wouldn't have asked, oh . . . I see . . . are
           you on't dole, then?

MAXINE   No.

SUZANNE   You're not stuck in a council flat with a baby and
            no money?

MAXINE   No.

SUZANNE   Well what then?

MAXINE   Why's it matter? I refuse to be . . . you know . . .
            what do I mean . . . categorized, that's it, by my
            job.

SUZANNE   Oh.

MAXINE   I work in a clothes shop, it's shit and the people I
            work with are all cunts.

            (SUZANNE *is gobsmacked to hear that word from a
            girl.*)

SUZANNE   Oh . . . I hate my life as well.

MAXINE   I didn't say that.

SUZANNE   Oh . . . I didn't mean it like that . . . sorry. Who cut
            your hair?

MAXINE   I did it myself. Do you want to come and sit with
            me, then you're not on your own . . . hating your
            life.

SUZANNE   Please. Where do you buy your clothes?

            (*A tune takes over, then fades out. The night is
            over, the 'house' lights come up, all are
            shattered.* MAXINE *sees* EUGENE, *ignores* SUZANNE'S
            question. As she walks past EUGENE, *he looks up
            to speak to her but she simply nods. He is
            speechless, completely shattered by the whole
            experience. At length he nods.*)

MAXINE   Well . . . alright mate, maybe I'll see you here
            another time or somat'? Dirty git. (*She goes.*)

EUGENE   Yeah . . . no . . . wait...

                (*But she's gone. He looks after her, longingly, in a dreadful state.*)

                Who are you? What's your name? Will I ever see you naked? Blow bubbles on your belly . . . twang your knicker elastic?

                (*Then* SUZANNE, *having seen how* MAXINE *does it, walks past him also, dead cool.*)

SUZANNE   Yeah right, see you mate . . . dirty git.

                (EUGENE *looks again, wondering who the hell she was.* MAXINE *turns to* SUZANNE.)

SUZANNE   I could ring you maybe, in the week.

MAXINE   We aren't on the phone. I live in Hulme, it's not safe for the engineers. The police only come when they've got air cover. I'll be here next week though.

                (SUZANNE *is chipper, she's made a friend. They exit.* EUGENE *ambles to the gents bog, where* DANNY *is doing early morning ablutions, changing T-shirt, brushing his teeth, etc.* EUGENE *undoes his trousers, feels about, gets slightly, then increasingly agitated.*)

EUGENE   Oh Jesus! What's happened here?

DANNY   What's up?

EUGENE   Nothing . . . Well . . . I can't . . . oh shit . . . I can't find it!

DANNY   Can't you?

EUGENE   No . . . it's not here . . .

DANNY   Keep lookin', it's gotta be in there somewhere.

EUGENE   It's not! It's fuckin' gone!

DANNY   Jesus! Nobody move! Don't sweep up!

EUGENE   I've hardly ever used it as well . . .

DANNY   Think back man, when did you last see it?

             (EUGENE, *still tripping, commences looking round
             the floor, shock-horror etched into his
             countenance.*)

EUGENE   I don't know.

DANNY   Come here, it's got to be in there somewhere . . .

             (DANNY *takes hold of him by the waist and
             pretends to assist in the search.*)

EUGENE   Lee! Mum! Dad! Any fucker! There's a strange
             man fiddling about in my trousers! Get off!

DANNY   I'm just trying to help, it's happened to me before
             now.

EUGENE   Has it? What did you do?

DANNY   (*laughs*) Waited, you soft git . . . it's the phet, the
             bombers . . . it's what it does.

EUGENE   Burns your knob off? That should be in
             government warnings! That's the sort of thing you
             should be taught at school!

DANNY   It'll be back by tomorrow . . . have you got any
             skins? Come on, I'll skin up. Danny, by the way.
             This your first time here?

EUGENE   And last if it's gonna end like this.

DANNY   No man, you'll be here again. Calm down . . . it's
             temporary.

EUGENE   It better be . . . Eugene . . .

(They leave the bogs. DANNY *commences skinnng up with some skins he finds at length in his own pocket. This next exchange should be nice and steady, like two guys relaxing after a blast of dancing, etc.)*

DANNY   What do you think people who don't come here . . . don't get it . . . what do you think they're doing with their lives?

EUGENE   Well let's think, it's ten past eight on Sunday morning, they're all nursing hangovers . . . getting up for church, my old man will be . . . or washing their cars.

DANNY   Aye, when they could be in Wigan looking for their knob.

EUGENE   And feeling like this! Oh man . . . I've never felt this good . . . northern soul . . . it's like . . . putting the lights on for me. Jesus Christ . . . I've been blind all my life . . . Danny . . . the whole of popular music as we know it . . . is bollocks!

DANNY   Aye . . . life in general with it. Far as I can work out this country shuts at ten o' clock. Except Saturdays . . . for us anyway, I love it . . . fuckin' love it . . . You see, Eugene, rhythm is everything to me. I do everything in rhythm. I eat, sleep, shite and piss in rhythm.

EUGENE   *(dead sincere)* I'm really pleased for you.

          (They enjoy a relaxing spliff. After a few seconds, or his first couple of tokes on it, EUGENE *leaps to his feet and lets a huge 'yahoo' shriek of joy, punching the air as in he who has just achieved beyond his wildest dreams, seen the light, found God, etc.* DANNY *laughs once more.)*

EUGENE   Danny . . . I want you to do something for me.

DANNY   Aye?

EUGENE   I want you to teach me to dance . . . like you
            dance.

DANNY   I see . . . you want to be a master of the northern
            dance floor, do you?

EUGENE   I do . . . if you'll teach me.

            (DANNY *laughs at him.*)

EUGENE   What? Don't bleedin' laugh at me!

DANNY   Damn it son, do you know what it takes to master
            the timing, the acrobatics, the rhythm, the majesty
            of the true northern soul dancer?

EUGENE   I'm willing to learn if you'll teach me!

DANNY   So you can show off to girls, be the big 'I Am',
            'King It', The Snake himself! Is that what it's all
            about?

EUGENE   I suppose.

DANNY   Don't blame you, that's why I took it up.

EUGENE   So you will?

DANNY   I can teach you . . . but it'll be hard, and often!

EUGENE   I expect nothing less.

DANNY   Meet me on Wednesday, the room above Horwich
            working men's club, six o'clock.

EUGENE   Oh shit . . . I am so fucking hammered!

DANNY   Aye, me with you, keep the faith man!

            (*The two of them laugh, and wander off in that
            post-night out haze. The night is over, the week
            commences. An Abba tune creeps in. Lights up on*
            MAXINE.)

MAXINE   Monday, Tuesday, every bloody day! The mind
          bending, spirit crushing tedium of standing by
          that cash till. This month's manager, before he
          gets sacked for dipping his frauding bent fingers
          in the till, tortures us with Elton John, Queen and
          fucking Abba!

          Watching, waiting, for a shoplifter, at least it
          breaks the monotony . . . usually kids who should
          be at school, but they don't want to be at school,
          same as I didn't . . . but I wonder now.

          (*Cut to* SUZANNE, *who is at the dry cleaners.*)

SUZANNE   Magazines . . . telling me how . . . telling me why.
          It's all in how you do a thing, you can head a lot
          of things off at the pass if you know what you're
          doing. It's all in how you do a thing . . .

          Style, grace, rhythm . . . Audrey Hepburn.
          Think how much that woman headed off at the
          pass . . . one look, subtle, stylish . . . I have to
          really drive it home to 'em,
          Audrey, nothing, with ease . . . one eye movement,
          it's done, he knows, bog off, forget it.

          Audrey Hepburn would have looked fantastic on
          the dance floor,
          Moving that beautiful sleek thing she had going
          on there to a sound so sweet, deep, bathed in
          emotion, but stylish emotion, class.
          I'll never be Audrey Hepburn.

          (*A tune takes over.* SUZANNE *ceases musing, and
          enters* MAXINE'S *space. She is in the shop.*)

MAXINE   What you doing here?

SUZANNE   It's Wednesday, dry cleaner's shuts at dinnertime.

MAXINE   I wish this dump did. But then I'd have to go
          home, so . . .

SUZANNE   Do you not like it . . . at home?

MAXINE   It's not that. We've got . . . problems in the family.

SUZANNE   Oh . . . what like?

MAXINE   You don't want to know.

SUZANNE   (*slowly*) I do.

MAXINE   (*laughing*) I know well you do but I aren't telling you. Believe me you don't.

SUZANNE   Are you going again? On Saturday?

MAXINE   How do you think I cope with being stood here all week?

SUZANNE   Can I come?

MAXINE   Suzanne . . . can I ask you a question? Why do you want to come?

SUZANNE   (*thinks*) To hear my favourite song, and dance to it . . . they don't play it anywhere else . . . 'Something Beautiful' . . . I've never felt anything like when I first heard that record. What did you think I were gonna say?

MAXINE   Don't matter what I think . . . but I know what you mean. There's a tune they play called 'Don't Turn Your Back On Me' . . . no man'll ever take me where that song does.

SUZANNE   Really? There won't be a man do more for you than that song?

MAXINE   Not for fully three and a half minutes, no. It's what I tell 'em all when they ask as well.

SUZANNE   I . . . do they . . . ask?

MAXINE   You know what lads are like.

(Evidently not too many ask SUZANNE. *Cut to*
DANNY *is putting* EUGENE *through his paces
learning the dances. Time and again* EUGENE
lands on his arse.)

EUGENE   Oh it's no bleeding use, I'll never get it!

DANNY   You will, but you need the discipline required . . .
            Northern soul dancing's not just about learning
            moves . . . it's about feeling them.

EUGENE   About feeling the music?

DANNY   And responding only to what you feel . . . in here.

EUGENE   Why aren't . . . why don't you have a girlfriend,
            Danny?

DANNY   Couldn't.

EUGENE   What do you mean . . . you couldn't?

DANNY   Deal with it. It'd get in the way of the scene, the
            nighters.

EUGENE   Well couldn't you fit it round 'em?

DANNY   When? Takes me all day to sort out gear, sort
            myself out, travel to Wigan, maybe not getting
            home till Sunday night if I go on all day some
            place else . . . Monday, forget it, Tuesday, forget
            it, Wednesday you're just starting to come round
            but you can't handle any stress, talking to people
            and shit. Thursday well you need to start sorting
            gear out again in case there's a problem with it on
            Friday and you need to start looking elsewhere.
            Friday you're just too excited waiting for it to start
            and Saturday! Man what a day . . . freedom.

EUGENE   Aye, but . . . a shag's always handy innit?

DANNY   I'm faithful . . . to this little baby.

(*He holds his right fist out,* EUGENE *inspects his own, nodding in agreement.*)

EUGENE   A true friend, I'm not disagreeing with you . . . but . . . company . . . do you not get . . . I don't know . . . lonely?

DANNY   No . . . I did have a bird . . . but she had to go.

EUGENE   Really? What did you say?

DANNY   I looked at her . . . and said . . . aye, okay love, if that's how you feel, I just hope you and him'll be very happy together.

EUGENE   Oh . . . she dumped you?

DANNY   For a full weight wanker, that's what . . . !

(*He stops himself, realizing he has just given the game away.*)

EUGENE   I er . . . see.

DANNY   Maybe you do, maybe you don't as well . . . come on, less talk.

(*Back to* SUZANNE *and* MAXINE *in the shop.*)

MAXINE   I don't think I'd like to go out with anybody at Wigan, anyway . . . get in the way of me dancing.

SUZANNE   Yeah, I'm the same . . . I've kind of got a chap anyway . . . if I want . . . he's called Graham, well he keeps asking to go out with me, I'm not bothered but he is.

MAXINE   Lucky you. And do you go out with him?

SUZANNE   No.

MAXINE   He can't be that nice then.

SUZANNE   Oh, he is . . . he really is, but . . . he's . . .

MAXINE   Pig ugly.

SUZANNE   No . . . well he isn't Robert Redford . . . but then
             who is, and he isn't Michael Greenhalgh either, no
             . . . he's really nice . . .

MAXINE   But he's no film star and he don't rock your boat
             . . . so let me guess, Graham is twenty . . . one?

SUZANNE   Twenty two.

MAXINE   And he's most of the way to being like your dad
             already.

SUZANNE   How did you guess that?

MAXINE   Men come in shapes, sizes and distinct types.
             Anyway you should be glad he's only most of it.
             My brothers aren't that old and they're old men
             already, beer, fags, telly. Apart from our Craig.

SUZANNE   What's he like?

MAXINE   Worse. When he's out . . . I don't know what's up
             with him, we were really close as kids but now . . .
             he just steals . . . vandalizes, steals again.

SUZANNE   Michael Greenhalgh to a tee.

MAXINE   Does Michael Greenhalgh inject heroin?

             (SUZANNE *is shocked at the very mention of that.*)

MAXINE   Yep . . . bang at it. He's emptied every saving jar
             and meter in the house, stolen stuff me mum's had
             all her life, me dad's barred him, but me mum lets
             him back in . . . our John, that's me other brother,
             goes berserk 'cos he's nicked stuff of his and
             throws him out again . . . Craig calls the police and
             says John assaulted him, me mum cries, me dad
             shouts at me mum, my mum goes to church, my
             dad goes to the pub, our John kicks the shit out of
             his girlfriend and she arrives round screaming,

usually at me mum. And I sit upstairs counting the fucking days till I can afford to live somewhere else.

SUZANNE   (*shocked*) Oh . . . I see.

MAXINE   You wanted to know.

SUZANNE   Our house in't like that.

MAXINE   Mine didn't used to be. So come on then, what's this Graham do?

SUZANNE   Somat' with ice cream.

MAXINE   What?

SUZANNE   Ice cream place, I don't know.

MAXINE   When I were little I always wanted to marry an ice cream man, then we'd never run out, do you know what I mean?

SUZANNE   Hmm, or the pop man. Would you like to get married?

MAXINE   No, not now.

SUZANNE   How do you know that, you might meet someone.

MAXINE   Might meet someone but I aren't tripping down any aisle with him, and that's that.

SUZANNE   Graham wants to marry me.

MAXINE   Has he asked you?

SUZANNE   No, but I know he does.

MAXINE   He might just want all the best bits that come with it but not the actual ring and pallava.

SUZANNE   Well he's barking up the wrong tree for that . . . have you . . . ever . . . are you . . .

MAXINE   Am I what?

SUZANNE   Have you ever done it? With a lad I mean?

MAXINE   No . . . not with a lad, just girls for me Suzanne.

SUZANNE   What!?

MAXINE   Having you on . . . course I have . . . have you?

              (SUZANNE *shakes her head warily.*)

SUZANNE   How . . . many?

              (MAXINE *starts to think back, we can see her
              doing numbers in her mind like it's going to be
              quite a few.*)

              There's this one girl I know, not Carol, this other
              girl, Yvonne, she's our age, 18, 19, I think it's a
              right scrubber's name that in't that, Yvonne, every
              Yvonne I've ever known's been a bit . . . Do you
              know what she told me?

MAXINE   About a dozen.

SUZANNE   (*cuts across her*) Eight! She's done it with eight!
              Basically every lad who's ever winked at her the
              slut, she's whipped 'em off there and then far as I
              can see. Go on, how many?

              (MAXINE *is revising her figure severely back down
              again.*)

MAXINE   Oh, er . . . just a couple . . . maybe three?

SUZANNE   Well is it two or three? Surely you'd know that.

MAXINE   It's two.

SUZANNE   How come two?

MAXINE   The first one . . . left me.

SUZANNE   (*sympathetic*) Soon as he'd had what he wanted,
            well that's your mistake you see.

MAXINE   Hmm . . . I do seem a bit error-prone in that area.

SUZANNE   Well, long as you've learnt your lesson. Anyway
            look at me stood here talking all day, so you're
            going on Saturday?

MAXINE   Yes, you?

SUZANNE   For deffo . . . I can't wait.

MAXINE   I might try and get my sister to come as well.

SUZANNE   Brilliant, do. What's she called?

MAXINE   Yvonne.

            (SUZANNE *is mortified. Back to* DANNY *and*
            EUGENE, *both are in a different T-shirt, ie it's
            another night. Another little dance step* DANNY *is
            teaching comes to a close.*)

DANNY   The northern scene, Wigan, it's not about chasing
            girls . . . it's about something . . . deeper,
            something more . . . spiritual, soulful, than any
            relationship . . . I am a maintenance man. Do you
            know what that means?

EUGENE   You er . . . maintain stuff.

DANNY   I do . . . but what it really means, is that Monday
            to Friday . . .
            I am a big fucking nothing . . . I have nothing . . .
            that's mine . . .
            That's special . . . that's unique . . .

            (*From here on as* DANNY *goes into this he is
            getting further and further wound up, beginning
            to freak* EUGENE *out.*)

I get up at the same time, I leave the house at the same time,
I put me snap in the same tupperware box.
Coat, boots, always the same, the only ones I have, part of me now, an extension of me skin, skin, there's another thing, what's that about? I tell you man, I'd never met a black bloke till I went to Wigan, straight up is that, or thought about it, you know . . . all that deep down ghetto . . . pain, you know, and the dog's fucked off and it's pissing down again . . . aye man, suffering . . . you know, Detroit, Philadelphia . . .

EUGENE   Bolton . . . Bradford . . .

DANNY   All of 'em, where it comes from . . . the whole . . . experience, you know what I mean? It's opened my eyes, I've learned more through this stuff than I ever got out of school and I'm not pulling your stick there either. Anyway where were we?

EUGENE   You were in Philadelphia, I were in Bradford . . .

DANNY   Oh aye . . . I walk the same route, past the same derelict shit, the same rows of concrete grey damp stained houses, in fairness it'd do me head in if I walked on one time and they'd all changed. In fact I'd freak at that.

EUGENE   Aye well, shall we crack on . . .

DANNY   I reach the yard at the same time, ten minutes before me shift starts. We have tea, me and Lionel and Arthur, both of whom are over a hundred years old but have somehow stolen the bodies of a thirty five and forty seven year old respectively. Both of whom may be dead but are blessed with the good fortune not to know it.

EUGENE   Shall I start the record again?

DANNY   I walk into the shed, say 'alright?', and they will scour their entire vocabulary, trawl their intellect, before replying . . . 'aye', and occasionally follow

it up with . . . 'could be worse, could be better,
could be dead'. Is it worse or better? Is it any
fucking different? We are maintenance men.

EUGENE   Right . . . I see . . . and what's your point like?

DANNY   Saturday . . . Wigan Casino . . . that's my point!
          I'm something . . . that's my time. My chance to
          live properly . . . for a few precious hours . . .
          You have to know what that means . . . feels like
          . . . to have the time, the energy, the determination,
          to master the steps.

EUGENE   I know what that feels like . . . I haven't chopped a
          chicken,
          De-boned a lamb, thrown a few kidneys in for free,
          or said,
          'Now then Mrs Dawson, how's your Bert!'
          'Fucked, Eugene, utterly fucked, thanks for
          asking.'
          In days without thinking of it . . . what it was like
          . . . the sounds . . . the smells . . . the speed . . .
          that girl . . . I don't even know her name.

DANNY   Forget her name, forget all about her . . . just
          dance.

EUGENE   I can't . . . I can't think of anything but her.

DANNY   It happened to us all first night we came.

EUGENE   What did?

DANNY   Girl across the dance floor . . . all that rhythm,
          sweet sexy movement.

EUGENE   And what did you do about it?

DANNY   Me? I copped off with her.

EUGENE   I thought you said it wasn't about that.

DANNY   I said it isn't about chasing them.

EUGENE   Yeah? And what happened like?

DANNY   Well, we went back to hers and . . .

              (*A series of nods, gestures, etc.*)

EUGENE   You gave her one?

DANNY   Damn right I did.

EUGENE   Who was she like, what happened to her?

DANNY   She still goes to Wigan, it's the same one you're
              after. Aye we've all had her, mucky little goer that
              one . . .

EUGENE   You what!?

              (DANNY *cracks out laughing.*)

              You bastard!

DANNY   Eugenc . . . everything comes to he who can back-
              flip in rhythm.
              You see the other guys out on the dance floor, it
              took them all months to learn that.

EUGENE   You mean they all practice?

DANNY   Course they do, they practice and practice so it
              looks easy, natural . . . then it's got soul.

EUGENE   I'll get there . . . I know I will . . . and when I do . . .

DANNY   She'll drop 'em.

EUGENE   In a flash.

DANNY   Won't know what's hit her.

EUGENE   Too right.

DANNY   No worries.

DANNY   She got any mates? Give us them skins . . . here,
           look what I've got as well . . .

           (*He picks up a record and shows it to* EUGENE.)

           'Looking For You', Garnett Mimms, twenty quid,
           that is a golden tune, believe you me.

EUGENE   Nice one. How many have you got, in your
           collection?

DANNY   Two hundred and eighty four with this one.

EUGENE   (*grabs it from* DANNY) Let's wang it on!

DANNY   (*horrified*) Oh I can't play it, worth too much to
           ever play it, might get scratched. It's like . . . a
           piece of heaven is that record to me.

           (DANNY *retrieves the record, holds and looks
           upon the record like a proud father would his
           first-born babe.* EUGENE *watches him a moment.*)

EUGENE   This stuff's pure addiction, isn't it?

DANNY   Northern? Once you get it . . . no going back.

EUGENE   I can't stop now man . . . I've started . . . and I
           can't stop.

DANNY   I know it.

           (*Both are slightly solemn, as if they are
           acknowledging some truly fundamental truth
           about themselves and the meaning of existence. It
           is emotional.*)

EUGENE   Is there any more gear in that bag?

DANNY   Aye, go easy though, it's got to top me up all
           week has that.

           (*Both crack out laughing. Music takes us into
           another sequence, the lads tip more speed into*

themselves, and dance all day. MAXINE *and*
SUZANNE *are in the space seperately, doing simple
little stuff, lay on a bed, reading a book, trying
on outfits for the weekend, etc.*)

SUZANNE   Wednesday night . . . Coronation Street's finished.
So that's that then . . . up to my bedroom . . . lark
about on my sewing machine . . .
Play my Gladys Knight record . . . and maybe my
Rod Stewart one.
I don't mention my Rod Stewart records when I'm
at Wigan.

DANNY   Aye . . . rhythm, rhythm, rhythm . . . the rattle roll
and mind blasting thuds of machine, steel, oil, dirt.
In far-off dank and shitty corners of the yard we
see the odd occasional rat and entertain ourselves
trying to get it in one with a suitably vicious lump
of brick. I've never hit one of the fuckers yet.

Each day the same. It'll be ten, maybe eleven
hours before I finish.
I do this five times a week. My whole life is
governed by it.
Rhythm. Some days I could lay on the ground and
cry.

*(And so Saturday arrives. All are readying
themselves.)*

MAXINE   Skirt, knee length, shoes, sensible, soft,
comfortable.
Tops, tight so there's no flying up and giving 'em
all a shot of what I've got . . . or haven't.
And another weekend has been safely reached.
Another week of boredom has been skilfully
trudged through.

SUZANNE   Knickers . . . medium size, I can't be doing with
them little stringy things that get lost up your
arse.

EUGENE   Shirt, Ben Sherman or Fred Perry, what's it to be?

DANNY   Trousers, baggy . . . shoes, slippy, essential.
             Bag . . . the crucial items, talc, Johnson's Baby
             Powder,
             Not Boot's own brand, can't skimp on a thing like
             that.
             And the special, crucial little compartment down
             the side,
             For the . . . aye, we needn't dwell any further . . .

SUZANNE   Saturday . . .

MAXINE   Saturday . . .

DANNY   Beautiful Saturday! When the whole world makes
             sense . . .

EUGENE   Oh the sheer fucking Saturday-ness of a good
             Saturday!
             It is impossible to describe the feeling in your
             veins
             At seven o' clock of a Saturday night as you sit in
             and wait for time to come round.
             The big bottle of phet sat under the sideboard,
             Waiting to whistle you off,
             An hour in the gym, pump some shit and go mad!
             Fight them fuckin' bars and bend the cunts!
             An hour in the shower . . .

             An hour on the bus, the train, a walk from the
             station.
             Caramba . . . quaff that phet and King Kong was
             fuck all!
             Away and fire in my rivers like Hiawatha and Crazy
             Horse, Geronimo, Arthur Scargill, and any other
             Tragic heroes you can think of who never stood a
             cat's chance, now you think of it!

             (*And so the big night is here.* EUGENE *is ready to
             dance in the very centre of the floor.*)

EUGENE   Danny . . . I'm here . . . I'm a Casino regular!

DANNY   I'm truly proud of you. Here, man . . . I've scored
             the best gear I've ever scored in my life, drop a

few bombs of that and thank God there's a roof or you'd fly straight out!

(DANNY *gives him the gear.* EUGENE *quaffs it, gurns a bit in swallowing it.*)

EUGENE   Oh man, how good is this gonna be!?

DANNY   Easy easy . . .

(*A tune comes in for him to start dancing to. He nods at* DANNY, *all set.*)

DANNY   You're on your own . . . fly boy wonder, fly like Eddie Holman can fly!

EUGENE   Oh God . . . I'm ready to go. Stand back y'all!

DANNY   And remember . . . ignore her completely, let the music enter your soul and the dancing do the talk brave Hiawatha.

(*Music comes in loud as* EUGENE *commences dancing in the most relaxed and free flowing fashion, hugely better than anything we have seen him do thus far, like he has pulled it all together.* MAXINE *and* SUZANNE *enter the space and see him. The screens and visuals should really enhance this, give us a real sense of him wizzing off his tits.*)

SUZANNE   Do you know him?

MAXINE   No.

(*Tracks come and go,* EUGENE *is now at a point of utter ecstatic hedonism, throwing himself full tilt into the dancing.* SUZANNE *and* MAXINE *dance somewhere near to him but he doesn't even see them, so far gone is he.* DANNY *is near at hand also. At length* DANNY *and* MAXINE *get talking.*)

MAXINE   Your mate's going for it.

DANNY   Eugene? Aye, well he's had a good teacher you
             see.

MAXINE   I think I spoke to him the other week.

DANNY   You might well have done, I wouldn't bother
             trying now like.

MAXINE   No he looks a tad far gone.

DANNY   Here, what did the bouncer say when a bloke
             walked into the nighter with a set of car jump leads
             round his neck?

MAXINE   What?

DANNY   You can come in as long as you don't start
             anything!

             (MAXINE *cracks out laughing at the gag,* EUGENE
             *looks up. Having nearly killed himself with his
             dance steps for her benefit all night, she is
             laughing and joking with* DANNY! *He is utterly
             galled and gobsmacked by it. The music comes
             back in louder but all* EUGENE *can see is* DANNY
             keeping MAXINE *in mighty good crack while he is
             a sweat-soaked wreck on the dance floor. Finally
             the music fades out and the lights come up,*
             EUGENE *is a shattered hollow shell of a man.*
             DANNY *comes over.*)

DANNY   Man you looked like you were loving that!

             (EUGENE *simply glares at him.*)

MAXINE   See you, we're going . . . (*To* EUGENE.) You okay,
             mate?

             (*She nods her cheerios to* DANNY *and shapes to
             leave. When* EUGENE *speaks he is breathless, his
             voice a husky drawl, she is almost offstage when
             at last he gets the strength to shout.*)

EUGENE   Wait! Please. Who are you? Will you be here next
            week?

MAXINE   I don't know . . . I have to go now.

EUGENE   Will you . . . how will I . . . see you again?

MAXINE   I don't know.

            (*He looks dejected, like he's getting the brush-
            off.*)

MAXINE   Is it so important?

EUGENE   Yeah . . . it is . . . to me.

            (*She considers a moment.*)

MAXINE   Why?

EUGENE   Because . . . it is.

            (*There is a moment's uncertainty.*)

MAXINE   So . . . what now?

EUGENE   I don't know.

            (*She kisses him on the cheek, and leaves him
            sitting there.*)

EUGENE   Oi . . . what's your name?

MAXINE   Maxine. I'm off for a cup of tea next door . . . you
            look like you could do with one.

            (MAXINE *exits.* EUGENE *collapses.* DANNY *comes
            over and commences reviving him.*)

EUGENE   What were in that fucking gear you gave me?

DANNY   Great stuff, isn't it? I didn't do any myself, it's too
            strong.

EUGENE   You what?!

DANNY   She's up for it, man. All the while she were talking
              to me, she were looking at you.

EUGENE   Me? Do you think?

DANNY   Aye . . . café . . . go.

              (EUGENE *stands. He is still twitching from all the
              gear he's had, trying to straighten himself out,
              etc, then sets off after* MAXINE. DANNY *sits down,
              commences rolling a spliff, alone again. He
              cracks out laughing, but he is alone and he
              knows it. Nice tune comes in to cover the hiatus,
              eg, Ray Pollard's, The Drifter.* SUZANNE *and*
              MAXINE *have cups of tea as* EUGENE *enters the café
              space. He sits down with them but has no idea
              what to do or say. They look at him curiously.*)

SUZANNE   Are you alright, love?

MAXINE   Conversation isn't your strong point, is it?

SUZANNE   Do you do gurnin' and stuff?

MAXINE   Suzanne!

SUZANNE   Well his face . . . it's like he's chompin' on
              walnuts or sheep shit or somat.

EUGENE   It is, actually.

MAXINE   What, a walnut or sheep shit? Let's see . . .

EUGENE   Conversation . . . it's a very strong point with me.
              But it has to be intelligent conversation.

              (*Both girls give an 'oooh!' response.*)

SUZANNE   Well, you're in't wrong place then.

MAXINE   No he isn't. So . . . what? It's just us you can't
              talk to?

EUGENE   I might not want to talk to you.

MAXINE   Just lick me?

            (*His face drops a degree.* SUZANNE *looks equally
            horrified.*)

MAXINE   I heard you loud and clear, mate.

SUZANNE   I didn't hear anything of the sort, what's all this?

EUGENE   Now and again . . . I'll . . . let myself down with
            my . . .

MAXINE   Dirty mind?

EUGENE   Honesty.

SUZANNE   (*alarmed*) What's this about?

MAXINE   That's a problem for you. It's whether it's the only
            one I'm worried about. I'm forming a picture . . . I
            don't know how accurate it is yet, though.

            (EUGENE, *aware that* SUZANNE *is present, doesn't
            really know what to say so comes directly to the
            point, taking a huge risk.*)

EUGENE   Will you come out with me on Saturday?

MAXINE   With you? Why would I want to do that?

EUGENE   Because . . . I want.you to. Because you dance
            beautifully and . . . I can tell you're not thick.

MAXINE   How can you tell?

EUGENE   I just . . . can . . . you've got . . . soul, Maxine . . .
            that's what you've got.

MAXINE   And you want to lick me.

EUGENE   That as well. Depends on the impression you make
             throughout the evening.

MAXINE   The impression I make?

             (SUZANNE *is positively rattled by this
             conversation.*)

SUZANNE   Cheeky swine!

MAXINE   Let's think . . . spend an evening in silence, apart
             from the odd three word, slightly weird, possibly
             very rude, exchange? What do you think,
             Suzanne?

SUZANNE   Steer well clear!

MAXINE   Hmm. Sound advice.

             (EUGENE *looks deflated.*)

MAXINE   So, I'll go with you . . . on one . . . no, two
             conditions.

EUGENE   Oh . . . and what are they?

MAXINE   The first is that you promise not to dance like a
             deranged lunatic all night. You must have put in a
             lot of practice though in fairness to you, you were
             rubbish first time you came.

EUGENE   Was I? And the second?

MAXINE   The second . . . is that you talk for a full minute.

EUGENE   A full minute?

MAXINE   Starting now.

             (EUGENE *is thrown by this and has no idea what
             to say.*)

EUGENE   Why?

MAXINE   'Cos I don't want to go out with somebody I don't
              think I can talk to.

EUGENE   Fuckin' 'ell . . . that's a bit steep . . . a full minute
              . . . a full minute . . . er . . . life's crap, Bolton's
              crap, me dad's an arsehole, United shouldn't have
              let George Best leave, punk rock's bollocks . . .

MAXINE   About you . . . I don't care about punk rock or
              George Best.

SUZANNE   George Best, drinker, Irish, it's what they're like.
              My mum says it's from all the wet weather and
              years of benediction.

EUGENE   You don't care about George Best!? Have you got
              no soul? What do you think about then? What is
              there in people's lives who don't like football and
              northern soul?

SUZANNE   Coronation Street, my sewing machine, The
              Onedin Line, do you watch that ever, Maxine?

MAXINE   Now and again, you're a football fan, shit. One
              minute, every time you cock up or get boring it
              starts again.

EUGENE   Soul music is the centre of everything, it's the
              reason, rhyme all of it.

MAXINE   About yourself . . . tell me about yourself, start
              again.

EUGENE   Jesus! Okay . . . I was born in Bolton, but I'll not
              die there.

SUZANNE   Not for a while anyway, please God.

EUGENE   Do you mind, this is my minute.

MAXINE   Don't snap at her.

EUGENE   Am I supposed to be talking or you two?

MAXINE   Well jazz it up then, dull as dishwater so far . . .

            (*He gives her a look, like 'okay, you asked for it',
            then sets off stream of consciousness style.*)

EUGENE   Eugene Drennan, son of Jim and Marian . . .
            My mam left home when I was twelve,
            Said she'd had enough, she went back to
            Blackpool,
            Where her people came from . . . she left me.
            She said she was leaving him not me and that
            she'd come back,
            But she was lying, she never came back.
            She died, in Blackpool.

            (MAXINE *didn't expect that.*)

            I remember nothing at all about school, except
            getting beaten shitless by a kid called Steven
            Wilcox because I kicked his football by accident
            And I had to go to hospital.
            I hardly ever went after the age of fourteen,
            And what went on before that went over my head,
            Apart from a project we did on aeronautical flight.

SUZANNE   Boring.

MAXINE   Carry on.

EUGENE   We made our own kite to prove the theory, that it
            works, you know.
            Some didn't see the point, arguing, perhaps
            correctly,
            That McDonald Douglas, Boeing and others had
            already

            Proved the theory so why should we when we can
            see planes in the
            Fucking sky all day long but I enjoyed it . . .
            I painted that kite . . . in the colours of the Navajo
            tribe . . .

MAXINE   Why the Navajo tribe?

EUGENE   Cos I like 'em.

MAXINE   Did they fly kites?

EUGENE   If they didn't they should have they'd have loved it.
          Hiawatha, what a man, he wasn't a Navajo, mind.
          I make my own tea, breakfast and dinner.
          For mash get smash.
          I've also mastered bubble 'n squeak
          And I can do amazing things with fish fingers.
          I wash my own clothes, iron my own shirts,
          Brutus, Ben Sherman, Sta-prest trousers only.

MAXINE   Goes without saying.

EUGENE   I know when to be in the house and when to be
          out of it.
          Weekends, a good time to be out of it,
          'Cos he'll be in it and sooner or later he comes
          home from the club,
          Steaming pissed again.
          He's a lot of things all week but he's never
          violent, rough,
          Pig-fuckin' ignorant but never violent, until the
          weekend.

          I'll give him his due mind, he's never relented, not
          once.
          Not even when I got nicked, aged thirteen . . .
          In a sports shop in Bolton, stealing football
          shirts . . .

SUZANNE   Michael Greenhalgh all over, I knew it, don't touch
          him with a barge pole, Maxine!

EUGENE   And when it all were done and dusted and the
          coppers brought me home . . . he near knocked me
          unconscious in front of 'em,
          And the copper said, that's right, just what he's
          short of.
          Then he didn't speak to me at all for weeks.

MAXINE   What happened to him?

EUGENE   He's still in Bolton, I still live with him.

MAXINE   And does he know how much you love him really?

EUGENE   What?

MAXINE   Have you never said any of this to him?

EUGENE   Don't do my head in.

MAXINE   You started it . . . should have heard yourself.

EUGENE   I have one mate called Lee, he's as weird as I am.

MAXINE   You've changed the subject.

SUZANNE   Is he a thief an' all? Your mate?

EUGENE   I have a chair called Geronimo . . .

MAXINE   Geronimo?

EUGENE   Yes . . . Geronimo . . . what's wrong with that?

MAXINE   Nothing.

EUGENE   Would you like to ride Geronimo?

              (*She considers, deliberates.*)

MAXINE   Your chair?

EUGENE   My scooter . . . chair!

MAXINE   You said chair, how am I gonna know!

EUGENE   Would you like a ride on Geronimo?

MAXINE   What girl wouldn't?

EUGENE   He's parked outside. Sorry, I got a bit maudlin there, did I do the full minute?

MAXINE   If you didn't I can't bear any more, thought I were
            gonna cry for a second. Why are you obsessed
            with red indians?

EUGENE   'Cos they lost . . .

SUZANNE   Oh, lovely.

EUGENE   But they had style, them bucks.

SUZANNE   Oh heck, he's off again . . .

EUGENE   And when they wanted rid of them,
            I've read this, it's important, pay attention
            Suzanne,
            They fucked 'em up with diseases,

MAXINE   (*sarcastic*) Oh they didn't?

EUGENE   And then they wiped out all the buffalo. When
            you want to kill an animal, you want rid of it, you
            destroy its' habitat, it'll die on its own then,
            probably out of depression.

MAXINE   God, that's really sad.

EUGENE   I'm glad you feel that way. There ain't a solitary
            buffalo left in my part of Bolton. Hence no native
            tribesmen. Fact.

MAXINE   Is it?

EUGENE   It is . . . soon there won't be a factory, a mill or
            fuck all else, either.

MAXINE   Does that sort of thing upset you?

EUGENE   Come join me, aboard Geronimo, Maxine.

SUZANNE   I wouldn't.

MAXINE   Do you ride bareback or do you have a saddle? Or
            can you do both?

(EUGENE *merely casts her a glance, winks,*
whatever. MAXINE *stands up to go with him.*
SUZANNE *is aghast and crestfallen.*)

SUZANNE   Don't do it, Maxine!

MAXINE   Suzanne, I love you to bits . . . but . . .

SUZANNE   (*gutted*) But . . . he's got a scooter.

EUGENE   Chair.

SUZANNE   Chair. I'll be fine . . . don't worry about me. There
           an't been anyone raped and murdered in this café
           in a long time.

MAXINE   Exactly, I'll see you next week . . . yeah?

           (SUZANNE *nods.* EUGENE *and* MAXINE *exit to the*
           scooter, leaving SUZANNE *alone for a few moments*
           with her cup of tea. DANNY *enters.*)

DANNY   Eugene gone? (*She nods.*) Mind if I join you?

SUZANNE   Not at all. Hiawatha and Minnehaha have
           buggered off to look for a buffalo . . . in Bolton.

           (*He sits calm and still where he is, deep in*
           thought.)

SUZANNE   What are you thinking about?

DANNY   Eh? Oh . . . nothing . . . nothing important . . . me
           drugs have worn off. Always start thinking about
           shit I ought not to when that happens.

SUZANNE   What like?

DANNY   Just . . . stuff. Come on, I'll walk you to the
           station.

           (*She gets up and slowly follows him, their journey*
           is a meander, across the stage.)

SUZANNE   Stuff that makes you sad?

DANNY   Sometimes. Stuff can do that. It's why I love
            coming here . . . always the same buzz, same
            friendly faces . . . yours among 'em.

SUZANNE   You've been here every time I've ever come here.

DANNY   Aye . . . that's me . . . I'm a very sad man.

SUZANNE   Are you?

DANNY   No, I just told you . . . I love it.

SUZANNE   I love it . . . but I'm not sure I want to live it.

DANNY   Ah well you see . . . doesn't feel like there's any
            option for me. Northern soul music . . . the nighter
            scene . . . it's cost me everything really, friends,
            girlfriends, parents . . . they look at me like I'm off
            my rocker . . .

SUZANNE   And are you?

DANNY   Well and truly I hope. In their terms anyway.

SUZANNE   My mum . . . since I've started coming here . . .
            when I get home on Sundays, looking shattered . . .
            she says it's like I'm not me any more.
            It upsets me sometimes . . .

DANNY   Aye. I can see that. The way I see it . . . for people
            like us . . . there's a danger, Suzanne.

SUZANNE   What?

DANNY   To die . . . without ever having . . . lived . . .
            touched . . . something better than a shovel or a
            lathe or . . . enlightenment. You know?

SUZANNE   Something Beautiful. Yeah . . . I think I do know,
            now.

DANNY   Aye ... and we're lucky, you and me, lucky ...
             you know? To have found it.

             (*Cut to* MAXINE *and* EUGENE, *outside the café and
             about to board Geronimo.*)

EUGENE   Are you ... in danger of becoming my girlfriend,
             Maxine?

MAXINE   Depends ... if this scooter's em ...

EUGENE   (*quickly*) Chair!

MAXINE   If this chair's embarrassing.

EUGENE   It's a long long way from embarrassing, Maxine.

MAXINE   And after we've had a ride I want to know about
             your mum ... if you want to tell me ...

EUGENE   I never normally ... maybe I will tell you ... but
             first, Geronimo!

             (*Projections of* EUGENE *and* MAXINE *aboard his
             scooter. 'Something Beautiful' plays, this is the
             start of* EUGENE *and* MAXINE'S *love affair. This
             sequence should have the effect of moving time
             and their relationship on. It ends with him lifting
             her off the floor to swing her round happily.*)

MAXINE   Gerroff, mad lad!

EUGENE   No! Come here! (*He kisses her, passionately.*)

MAXINE   What the hell's got into you!

EUGENE   You have, right into my soul baby, like Dean
             Courtney ...

MAXINE   Is he in your soul? What haven't you told me,
             Eugene?

EUGENE   You're my castle in the sand ...

MAXINE   Am I?

EUGENE   That's right, it don't need no bricks to make it
              stand,
              'Cos you're my baby! Can't you see . . .

MAXINE   Is that right?

EUGENE   It is . . . Hence my latest brilliant idea! I want you
              to come and live with me.

              (MAXINE *is silenced by that. She deliberates.*
              Jump cut to SUZANNE *and* MAXINE.)

SUZANNE   Oh, I wouldn't do that!

MAXINE   You wouldn't?

SUZANNE   Not without getting married.

MAXINE   Ah well you see, I wouldn't do that without
              having lived with him.

SUZANNE   What if it don't work out?

MAXINE   Exactly, if it don't work out I can always move out
              again, no hassle no big deal but if you're married.

SUZANNE   Yeah, but if you're married you've got to make it
              work, haven't you?

MAXINE   Oh right, so the reason to get married is so that
              you can stick with it through thick and thin
              choose how unhappy you both are?

SUZANNE   That's what my mum says, good times and bad.
              All this living with this one, that one and the
              minute something goes wrong that's it, up sticks
              and onto't next one. It's why society's breaking
              down, look at all these strikes, people do as they
              like, children don't know right from wrong and
              they've got lesbians on the rates in London.

MAXINE   Have they?

SUZANNE   They will have, won't they? I just think . . . you
           should be careful.

MAXINE   I prefer to go by what my mum said.

SUZANNE   What's that?

MAXINE   Men . . . they're like bog roll.

SUZANNE   Are they?

MAXINE   Yeah. All you do is pull 'em off then wipe your
           arse with 'em.

           (*Both laugh.*)

SUZANNE   Did she really say that?

MAXINE   No did she hell, daft cow! She should have,
           though.

           (*Cut to* DANNY *and* EUGENE, *sat sifting through
           records like at* DANNY'S *house.*)

EUGENE   We're moving in together.

DANNY   (*not listening*) Sound one. Have you heard this?
           (*Passes him a record.*) Skin up another . . .

EUGENE   Baltimore and Ohio Marching Band? Condition
           Red . . . is it instrumental?

DANNY   What? Oh that yeah, it's amazing, I'll put it on in a
           minute. What you looking for?

EUGENE   What've I done with them skins? I said I'm moving
           in with Maxine.

DANNY   I heard you, good one, aye, oh, I've got 'em here
           . . . (*The skins.*) I still haven't stopped wizzing
           from Saturday, have you?

EUGENE   No. I were at it till midnight Sunday . . . I couldn't
           fucking move Monday, or yesterday . . .

DANNY   Only a couple of days to go, then we can do it all
           again! I tell you man, if I see a copy of 'I
           Surrender', Eddy Holman no matter what it costs
           I'm getting it. Man, I can die tomorrow as long I
           own that record . . .

           (*He sings a snatch of the song,* EUGENE *joins in.*)

           What am I supposed to be doing here? Oh aye,
           skinning up . . .

           (*Cut to* MAXINE *and* SUZANNE, *who looks slightly
           alarmed, then sad.*)

MAXINE   What's up?

SUZANNE   Nothing . . . well . . . you're moving in with your
           boyfriend and he's really cool and can dance and
           has a scooter . . .

MAXINE   Suzanne, it's a chair!

SUZANNE   Sorry, and you're gonna be really happy . . . and
           look at me.

MAXINE   Oh, don't say stuff like that, Suzanne . . . I love
           Eugene, I do . . . but I've told you about our house
           and . . . all the shit that goes down . . .

SUZANNE   Yeah.

MAXINE   I don't know if this is right either but . . . be happy
           for me . . . and you've got Graham, anyway.

SUZANNE   Hmm. Thing is, I share him with a sofa and Burnley
           FC . . . I've told him I'll have sex with him next time
           they win . . . way they're going on I might have to
           turn out for 'em myself. He took me to watch 'em
           once . . . says he'll do it again if I annoy him.

MAXINE   But he loves you . . . come here. (*They hug.*) Is it this light or have you put weight on?

(EUGENE *comes in. He puts his hands over* MAXINE'S *eyes, walks her forward a few paces, then removes his hands so she can see the flat he has rented for them. This can be created simply by means of an old sofa, a lamp, something very simple.*)

MAXINE   (*mock romantic*) Oh Eugene . . . it's an utter shithole!

EUGENE   I know baby, that's why I need you. I'd be out of my mind with depression on my own, wouldn't surprise me if there isn't cockroaches when you look . . .

MAXINE   When who looks?

EUGENE   When we look. At least it's our shithole, Max . . . you and me . . . forever?

MAXINE   Forever . . . does this really mean you love me more than Geronimo?

EUGENE   No.

(*She attacks him playfully, happy happy times, then exits. He is left alone on stage a moment, in the spot where he was at the beginning of the play.*)

EUGENE   Aye . . . the happiest times I ever knew . . . Wigan Casino . . . and Maxine . . . and I had 'em both. Perfection.

(*The lights fade. Music plays.*)

ACT TWO

DANNY *is round at* MAXINE *and* EUGENE'S *flat, deeply disgruntled. The Who's 'My Generation' is playing.*

DANNY   Quadro-shitey-phenia! Fuckin' mods and their pissy parkas on their clip clip two-stroke bastard Lambretta's! Eugene . . . for the sake of our friendship . . . you've got to ditch the chair . . .

EUGENE   Geronimo?

DANNY   No self-respecting northern soulie can dare to be associated with those shitheads! Kill 'em I would, with me own bare hands! Bastards turning up to Wigan and asking for fucking ska records! Ska records!

EUGENE   Easy tiger!

MAXINE   Oh no . . . I love Geronimo! How else will we get to Cleethorpes? Morecambe bay?

EUGENE   I don't know sweetheart . . . but he's right, it's got to go.

MAXINE   What?

DANNY   Do it Eugene. Now!

EUGENE   He's right . . . I can't be associated with mod revivalists, it . . . it's just wrong, angel . . .

MAXINE   Why does it matter?

EUGENE   Maybe it's a bloke thing sweetheart, just . . .

MAXINE   Maybe it is . . . when other boys shouted 'fuck off' at the bus conductor on the way home from school is that why you did it?

EUGENE   No, it was always me first then everybody else . . .
            what's your point?

MAXINE   Eugene . . . Geronimo . . . God, you are so shallow
            at times, a few mods turn up and that's that, you
            have to ditch the scooter . . .

EUGENE   Chair darling, chair . . .

MAXINE   I'll stick the chair up your backside! You worked
            hard to buy that scoo . . . chair! You saved all
            your butcher-boy money to buy it, you've never
            stopped polishing it since the day I met you . . .

EUGENE   Exactly, so a bit of sympathy wouldn't go amiss
            now that the time's come!

MAXINE   But it's why the time's come, don't you see that?
            You love that scooter, it's part of you . . . part of
            us . . . the first time we ever went out . . .
            everything we've ever done . . . together . . .
            Geronimo was . . . right beneath us.

EUGENE   And beside us . . . Saddleworth moor, summer '78,
            you gripped tight on the handle bars, me . . .

MAXINE   We're not alone!

EUGENE   We weren't then, you didn't bother, though . . .

MAXINE   I can't believe you're gonna just dump him . . .
            poor Geronimo.

EUGENE   It's like Danny says, angel . . . these mods . . .
            they're everywhere . . . first a few came . . . then
            more . . . and more . . . with their dire pop music
            and parkas . . . now the plains . . .

MAXINE   Oh, bog off the plains!

EUGENE   Sweetheart, Minnehaha . . .

MAXINE   Get stuffed. You know what you are?

EUGENE   Horny, it drives me wild when you get mad . . .

MAXINE   A poser.

            (*At that he is truly stunned. This is a very bad
            thing to say to a northern soul devotee.*)

EUGENE   I'm a what?

MAXINE   You're a vacuous, shallow poser.

EUGENE   Now damn and . . . damn shag it Maxine, what the
            fuck kind of a thing is that to say to a man like me?

MAXINE   It's the truth . . . That chair is . . . you . . . or it's
            the you I know . . . sod fashion, this trend or that
            one . . . I don't give a monkey's about all that
            crap, truth be told . . . it bores me shitless actually,
            which record's a girl's record, which record's true
            northern and which is wah wah wah, yawn yawn
            yawn . . .

DANNY   Jesus Christ, well I've heard it all now . . . Girls . . .
            they shouldn't be let in all-nighters, waste of good
            floor space . . . I'm gonna get off, I'll see you
            Saturday, Eugene . . .

            (DANNY *exits the flat in a strop.*)

EUGENE   Now look what you've done . . . embarrassed me in
            front of Danny!

MAXINE   Oh my God . . . I haven't, have I? Well . . . can you
            ever forgive me? I mean . . . Eugene . . . losing face
            . . . a moment when the armour cracked . . .

EUGENE   Maxine . . . I am not riding round on my chair
            knowing that people are looking at me thinking I'm
            one of those mod revivalist wankers and that is
            that and if you don't see the importance of that
            well . . . God help your soul. My final words on the
            matter.

MAXINE   Are they really?

EUGENE   Yes! I have spoken! Enough.

            (*She looks at him like he's truly off his head.*)

MAXINE   You're off your head!

EUGENE   Here's the proof, I live with you. I'm off out.

            (*He exits. Cut to* SUZANNE, *who was not onstage previously, and* MAXINE. *This scene can occur either in the flat or a separate area of the stage.*)

SUZANNE   It's only a scooter, Maxine.

MAXINE   It's not only a scooter. It's not.

SUZANNE   What's wrong?

MAXINE   You know it's weird . . . but . . . my whole life is Eugene . . . All-nighters . . . mates from the scene . . . I've let everyone and everything else fall by the wayside.

SUZANNE   That's 'cos you're not interested in them . . . like it or not.

MAXINE   Hmm. Maybe so . . . do you enjoy working at the dry cleaners?

SUZANNE   Yeah . . . it's ace . . . I love it . . . I live for it . . . no man'll ever make me feel like the smell of chemical cleaning agent wafting up from a well-cut cloth does, Maxine . . .

MAXINE   Don't take the piss.

SUZANNE   Well ask a proper question then! Do I enjoy working at the dry cleaners, I might not be Bamber Gascoigne but I aren't brain dead, either!

MAXINE   I . . . I hate the shop . . . I hate it, Suzanne . . . but the first time I ever walked down that meat market to meet him after work and saw him . . . in his

stripey apron, white coat, disgusting, blood-
splattered . . . he didn't see me . . . he were talking,
surprise surprise, laughing, big side of bacon over
his shoulder . . .

SUZANNE   Danish or English?

MAXINE   No idea, I could have ripped the lot off him and
thrown him down on that tray of liver and
sausages, briskit . . .

SUZANNE   Pork loin . . .

MAXINE   Exactly . . . and when he were finished . . . we went
for a burn on Geronimo . . .

SUZANNE   A what?

MAXINE   A burn . . . Eugene never rides . . . he goes for a
burn . . . we'd have been quicker walking but I
loved every second of being sat behind him . . .

SUZANNE   Sounds like you enjoyed a good few sat in front of
him as well . . .

MAXINE   Oi. Don't tell him this but I've had all my best
orgasms on that East Lancs road at thirty mile an
hour . . . downhill anyway.

SUZANNE   He worships you . . .

MAXINE   Hmm . . . nearly as much as he worships himself.
Now he's too cool to work at the meat market . . .
he's too cool for Geronimo. How's Graham? See
you think you're missing out, but I'd give either
arm for Eugene to get down off his high horse and
just admit he's an ordinary bloke . . .

SUZANNE   Yeah. Graham's . . . fine.

MAXINE   That all?

SUZANNE   Well . . . Burnley have a lot of injuries at the
moment, things are piling up on him a bit, if they

don't win this weekend they're back in the bottom three so . . .

MAXINE   Yeah . . . it we're on the news.

(The girls remain alone and pondering a moment further. EUGENE *is also alone, a suitably painful tune as he wanders in his wilderness.* DANNY *approaches, he either says or some means of a newspaper headline being projected tells us, 'Wigan Casino Closing down – September 19th, 1981 – the end of an era.')*

*(*EUGENE *is alone in the flat as* MAXINE *comes back to him.)*

EUGENE   Maxine it's only a scooter . . .

MAXINE   Chair!

EUGENE   Whatever . . . it's gone now . . . I sold it to a dealer in Horwich . . . be some twonk in a parka sat on it right now probably . . . poor old Geronimo . . .

MAXINE   Poor old Eugene, more like.

EUGENE   You know . . . you mean more to me than anything else in the world, don't you? It's only a scoo . . . chair, Maxine.

MAXINE   It's not only a chair . . .

(She turns and goes. He ponders a moment.)

EUGENE   Birds. Fuckin' mental.

(A new tune comes in, lights change as the Casino lighting reasserts itself. EUGENE *returns to the spot he had at the very beginning. We have arrived back at that point, the beginning of the last ever all-nighter at the Casino. From here on the action is all in the here and now, so to speak.)*

EUGENE   So . . . here we are. As I said, did it really . . . really
         happen? Wigan Casino . . . the former Empress
         Ballroom, 1973 to now. 1981.

         (*As at the start* DANNY *is awaiting him selling
         some gear.*)

DANNY   Eugene, are you selling me any fucking gear or
         what?

EUGENE   In a minute, give us a fuckin' chance.

         (EUGENE *goes to his bag, begins to rummage
         through as if he is searching for it, then very
         circumspect, all nods and winks, tries to slip it to*
         DANNY *without* MAXINE *seeing.*)

MAXINE   Not remotely suspicious. Just get on with it, no
         one's looking.

DANNY   Aye.

         (EUGENE *places the gear into the top of* DANNY'S
         bag. MAXINE *gives him a look.*)

EUGENE   What?

MAXINE   Nothing.

DANNY   What do I owe you?

EUGENE   Fiver.

DANNY   (*gives him the cash*) So . . . all up for one last fling
         then? (*Neither speaks.*) Aye . . . me the same . . .
         ought to be a cracker.

MAXINE   Let's hope so.

DANNY   Yep.

         (*He realizes there is tension between* EUGENE *and*
         MAXINE, *decides to get out of there.*)

DANNY   Aye well, I'll er . . . shoot up the record bar . . . see
             if I see anyone I know . . . aye, good idea, okay
             then . . .

             (DANNY *exits.*)

EUGENE   Do you have to do stuff like that?

MAXINE   Like what?

EUGENE   Deliberately make a fool out of me in front of my
             mates?

MAXINE   It isn't me does that.

             (SUZANNE *comes up to them.*)

SUZANNE   Found you! Everyone alright?

MAXINE   Yeah . . . are you?

SUZANNE   No.

MAXINE   Come and sit with us . . . are you okay?

SUZANNE   No.

MAXINE   What's up?

SUZANNE   I know it's the last night and everything . . . and I
             want to be cheerful, but . . . Maxine, I've . . . just
             come from the doctors.

MAXINE   And?

SUZANNE   . . . I've got a terminal illness.

EUGENE   Oh, Jesus.

MAXINE   (*gobsmacked*) Suzanne . . ?

             (SUZANNE *looks at her a long moment, then breaks
             it.*)

SUZANNE   (*softly*) Aw, would you really have been that upset
          if I had? Aw that's really lovely! I would if you
          were dying . . .

          (SUZANNE *commences hugging her, etc.*)

          We'll be friends forever, won't we?

EUGENE   What!?

MAXINE   You've just given me heart failure there!

SUZANNE   We will . . . Won't we?

MAXINE   Unless I kill you in the meantime.

SUZANNE   Obviously. Now come on you two, no being
          maudlin, this is our last night and we're all gonna
          have a good one. Right? . . . Exactly. Yep. Good-O.
          Well, I'll . . . wander off . . .

          (*Maybe not then, as neither respond.* SUZANNE
          *stands around a second or two, then goes. Music
          comes in, the night commences in earnest, we see
          both* DANNY *and* SUZANNE *dancing seperately.*
          EUGENE *and* MAXINE'S *conversation begins under
          the music, then as the music fades out we hear the
          dialogue from this point on.*)

MAXINE   I want to live . . . Eugene, more than Wigan Casino
          . . . nighters . . . and drugs.

EUGENE   Yeah.

MAXINE   I catch a bus down Oxford Road past the
          university and see all that stuff and people who
          look like they're going places every day and I go
          to a crappy shop in town and it depresses the shit
          out of me some days.

EUGENE   Quit.

MAXINE   What?

EUGENE   Quit the job. Bollocks to it. Don't be afraid . . .
          Maxine, you've got a brain . . . you could do
          anything.

MAXINE   I can't.

EUGENE   Can.

MAXINE   Can't.

EUGENE   Well don't say it's me stood in your way, I've told
          you.

MAXINE   Except you have me out all hours all weekend long
          and I don't get no sleep so I aren't in any nick to
          go and do anything or think of anything except
          just existing.

EUGENE   And dancing. What are you saying?

MAXINE   That . . . it'll do us good, when this place shuts . . .
          it'll be a chance for us to do other things . . .
          explore other avenues . . . do you think?

EUGENE   What like?

MAXINE   Oh forget it.

EUGENE   Let's think, we could take up potholing, that'd get
          us out in the fresh air, go camping.

MAXINE   What? You? In a tent? What if your shoes got
          muddy, you'd cry!

EUGENE   Teepee, Maxine! Teepee . . . little piebald pony
          tethered up, some bloke just out of sight playing
          the little pipey whistley flute thing . . .

MAXINE   Oh, I could grow my hair and put beads in it . . .

EUGENE   That's it, the little papooses running amok . . .

MAXINE   The what?

EUGENE   Well a dog, then. No, you'd be just about to give
              birth, alone, as the cavalry stalked then shot me
              out in the wheat field I'd planted . . . Burt
              Lancaster and Jean what'sername, Simmons?
              Peters?

MAXINE   Great. Eugene, why does your every flight of
              fantasy end in your being killed heroically, and me
              up the duff up a mountain?

EUGENE   Poetry!

MAXINE   Poverty. Why can't we have one where I end up
              earning thirty grand a year, stepping out of a
              sports car? Little Armani number, Farrah Fawcett
              Majors style?

EUGENE   You haven't got the knockers for it and besides
              where would I be in that one?

MAXINE   Parking the car, darling! Get you a little peaked
              cap.

EUGENE   Get out of here, no, better to go in one final blast
              of mayhem . . .

MAXINE   You see, for this mountain side I read tower block,
              and for the cavalry, I see drug squad kicking the
              door in at dawn to drag you off to Strangeways . . .

EUGENE   The reservation.

MAXINE   I don't want to live that way.

EUGENE   Women don't get it . . . always have to think on
              the bleak side . . .

MAXINE   Always have to think on the 'sorry mam can I
              come back home, I'm up the stick and my lovely
              boyfriend, well he just got six years but I love him
              and I always will' side . . . yeah right, mate, not
              likely!

EUGENE   I'll always love you.

MAXINE   I'll take that down to Tesco's, shall I?

EUGENE   Ah you're straightenin' my spin babe, I got to go . . .

MAXINE   Eugene! I'm serious.

            (*He goes to dance. Cut to* DANNY *and* SUZANNE,
            *she has gravitated to his side, he is having a
            breather, enjoying the music.*)

SUZANNE   I've . . . always thought one of these nights you
            and me'd get talking.

DANNY   We have done.

SUZANNE   No we haven't . . . not properly. We've exchanged
            about eight words about eight times.

DANNY   Ah well . . . I'm a man of few words.

SUZANNE   Hmm. What will you do next week?

DANNY   Decorate.

SUZANNE   What?

DANNY   Decorate.

SUZANNE   Why?

DANNY   It's what I do when I've got energy and no nighter
            to go to.

SUZANNE   I see . . . what do you decorate?

DANNY   My room.

            (*She begins to look brassed off, like she's making
            the effort and he isn't responding.*)

            I paint the walls a different shade to some tunes, it
            relaxes me.

SUZANNE   Do you live with your mum and dad still?

DANNY   Aye.

SUZANNE   How old are you, if you don't mind me asking?

DANNY   Old enough to know better.

SUZANNE   Than what?

DANNY   Than lots of stuff.

SUZANNE   And you still live at home?

DANNY   Yep.

SUZANNE   Don't that depress you?

DANNY   No.

SUZANNE   Why not?

DANNY   'Cos it don't, you a copper?

SUZANNE   No.

DANNY   Just wondered, all these questions, like. Where else am I gonna live?

SUZANNE   Your own place, bachelor pad . . .

DANNY   Tiger-skin bedspread, mirrored ceiling . . . mice.

SUZANNE   Exactly. I mean a flat, a girlfriend, get married . . . all the stuff people do.

DANNY   You got your own place?

SUZANNE   No . . . but I will have soon.

DANNY   I aren't interested in any of that.

SUZANNE   Aren't you? . . . just northern soul . . . nighters . . . and decorating?

DANNY   And the dog, I walk the dog. (*She looks blank.*)
           Actually it's a euphemism.

SUZANNE   What is?

DANNY   Walk the dog.

SUZANNE   I'm not with you, what's a euphemism?

           (*He cracks out laughing at her, always another
           question.*)

SUZANNE   Sorry, I'm from Burnley, you can't use big words.

DANNY   Well . . . when I say I'm off to walk the dog, what I
           mean is I'm off up the hill for a spliff . . . there's
           loads of us do it . . .

SUZANNE   Walk up the hill for a spliff?

DANNY   With the dog . . . round where I am there's more
           drug addled dogs than blokes, it's terrible . . .

SUZANNE   What?

DANNY   I'm having you on . . . but walk the dog means nip
           out for a jay.

SUZANNE   So you don't have a dog really?

DANNY   (*laughing*) Fuckin 'ell! Yes, but . . .

SUZANNE   Well how'm I gonna know? Oh I'm sorry, ignore
           me.

DANNY   Why would I want to ignore you?

SUZANNE   You do most times.

DANNY   That's me, not you.

SUZANNE   Do you not like people?

(*He looks at her sharply, freaked out by that.*)

DANNY   You've done my head in there, where's that come
           from?

SUZANNE   Don't know . . . you just seem closed in, shut off.

DANNY   It's called being stoned off your head.

SUZANNE   Is that all it is?

           (*He shakes his head, looks away into the nether
           distance like he is switching off from her already.
           Music comes in as the two of them stand
           awkwardly now. Music fades out again.*)

SUZANNE   That it? We've had us eight words?

DANNY   I counted fifty at least. I'm sorry . . . tonight's a . . .
           funny night.

SUZANNE   And you're a funny bloke . . . I meant what will
           you do when there's no Wigan?

DANNY   Don't know . . . might give it a break for a bit.
           What will you do?

SUZANNE   Loads of stuff, might get married.

DANNY   You got anyone in mind?

SUZANNE   Yes. This lad in Burnley.

DANNY   Does he know about this?

SUZANNE   It's all he wants from life.

DANNY   To marry you?

SUZANNE   What's wrong with that?

DANNY   Nothing. I envy you.

SUZANNE   No you don't. Will you never get married?

DANNY   Maybe . . . one day.

SUZANNE   Who to?

DANNY   My wife.

SUZANNE   Ha ha. Her name, I mean anyone in particular?

DANNY   Her name . . . Mrs Corcoran.

SUZANNE   Oh, get lost then!

DANNY   Well, as I've told you I haven't met her how am I
           gonna know her name?

SUZANNE   Am I . . . am I difficult to talk to?

DANNY   Crucifying. No, dead easy.

SUZANNE   I'm not boring?

DANNY   I didn't say that, but you're not hard to talk to.

SUZANNE   If . . . you knew me better . . . I'd be harder to . . .
           deal with.

DANNY   Would you? Best keep it at a distance then. Why
           would you be harder?

SUZANNE   Just would . . . the lad who wants to marry me . . .
           Graham . . .

DANNY   You're a total bitch to him, are you? You do right
           . . . it's what he wants you to be or he wouldn't
           put up with it. He loves it. What he really wants is
           you to take over his life and run it for him 'cos he
           hasn't a clue what to do with it himself.

SUZANNE   How do you know that?

DANNY   It's blokes. What they're like . . . plenty of 'em
           anyway. He might not say it, or even realize it
           but . . .

SUZANNE   It's true. Why aren't you like that then?

DANNY   The nighters. They're just too good to let go,
            know what I mean? You could never have a wife
            and do all that and be true to the scene as well.

SUZANNE   Do you really mean all that?

DANNY   (*laughing*) No, do I hell.

SUZANNE   I think you do mean it . . . it's like you said about
            other blokes . . . the nighter scene runs your life
            'cos you haven't a clue what to do with it yourself
            . . . you might not know it or even realize it . . .

DANNY   Oh, I think I do know it . . . I'm just happy with it.

SUZANNE   Are you? Really?

            (*He reflects a moment, perhaps he isn't so happy
            with it, truth be told.*)

DANNY   Time to dance, come on . . .

SUZANNE   Where?

DANNY   The floor.

SUZANNE   With you?

DANNY   Not if you don't want to. I'm not . . . you know . . .
            I know you've got your man in Burnley.

SUZANNE   I've never seen you dance with anybody . . . I've
            never seen anybody at Wigan dance with
            anybody.

DANNY   Tonight's a funny night, I told you that.

SUZANNE   It's weird, never mind funny.

            (*We watch them dance together, it should be
            beautiful, a sense of the last dance on the*

Titanic. Cut to EUGENE *and* MAXINE.)

EUGENE   I'll get a job and get myself sorted if that's what you want.

MAXINE   If that's what I want? Why would what I want have to surround you?

EUGENE   Well . . . I thought you wanted me to straighten out . . . I'm saying I'll do it.

MAXINE   Eugene, the drugs, dealing, we've let that become the big thing between us but . . . (*She stops.*)

EUGENE   But what?

MAXINE   (*very tentative*) I don't know if it is really . . . or the only thing.

EUGENE   Look once I get sorted, I know you want . . . to move on . . .

MAXINE   Really? So you'll stop laying in bed till four in the afternoon then wizzing off your tits playing northern tunes and smoking draw till six in the morning . . .

EUGENE   Sweetheart, I have to unwind now and again . . . you know that. One kiss . . .

(*He puckers his lips, shuts his eyes.*)

MAXINE   No.

EUGENE   One . . . here . . . go on . . .

(*In the end she has to laugh and gives him a kiss.*)

You look amazing tonight, do you know that?

(MAXINE *simply exits, leaving* EUGENE *alone as the music comes in good and strong.* EUGENE *looks around the dance floor, sees* DANNY, *wanders over.* DANNY *leaves* SUZANNE *to commence talking to* EUGENE.)

DANNY   Look at it . . . everyone busting their arses trying to get off on it.

EUGENE   Knowing full well it's fucked for us now well and truly.

DANNY   I don't want to deepen the gloom.

EUGENE   Do it, it's that kind of night.

DANNY   Okay then, I lost my job . . . well, we're shutting down.

EUGENE   Oh . . . is that bad?

*(*DANNY *looks at him a long moment.* EUGENE *simply doesn't get it, anything, apart from the northern scene and drugs.)*

DANNY   It will be in a month or so when I'm flat broke . . . taking the dog for a walk everyday and that's about it . . . my life.

EUGENE   You'll still have the nighters.

DANNY   *(ironic)* Yeah.

EUGENE   Well then.

DANNY   My whole life . . . it's had a routine, a rhythm a . . . routine! A plan!

EUGENE   Mine hasn't . . . still hasn't . . . won't ever have.

DANNY   You have Maxine, you have all that to do.

EUGENE   Yeah . . . I have Maxine. I don't . . . have a job 'cos I can't fucking handle 'em . . . when I worked on the meat market, it were only temporary . . . I never believed it were me, you know?

DANNY   Who was it, Mickey Mouse?

EUGENE   Tee hee . . . don't know who it was . . . if I went
             back there now I'd go mad. Can't believe I didn't
             at the time . . . it were only until something else,
             better, came along.

DANNY   Now it has, selling gear?

EUGENE   You see any other options let me know.

DANNY   Fuck off! I never wanted something else . . . I've
             loved every minute of this. Job, Wigan, building
             up to the weekend, coming down off it . . . perfect
             rhythm, all of it . . . everything fitted, had it's
             place, it's time. I had a job!

EUGENE   Come in with me, man . . . the two of us, a team . . .

DANNY   No way.

EUGENE   You're not thinking, look around you, man!
             Demand's red hot and getting bigger, constant,
             it's the coming thing believe me, folk are starting
             to see, daily life, job, grind, job, grind . . . Bullshit.
             There's a lot of openings for the right sort of
             bloke . . .

             (DANNY *is looking at his feet, clearly
             disapproving of everything* EUGENE *is saying.*)

             If you tell me it's got no honour I'll throw up.

DANNY   It hasn't.

EUGENE   Look, you were the one who told me all week long
             you're a big fucking nothing! This place, Wigan
             fucking Casino, the weekend, that's all you lived
             for . . .

DANNY   No weekend without the week, is there!

             (DANNY *gets irritated with him, close to punching
             him. Instead he simply moves away, leaving*

EUGENE *alone. Suddenly* EUGENE *starts clapping his hands, and giving it plenty.*)

EUGENE Come on you fuckers! Smile! DJ, give us somat to fucking smile about then! Don't sit down! Get up! Dance! What's the song say, dance! Dance! Dance! This is the last night of our fucking lives, the end of the world as we know it, we haven't a job or a clue between us but we're all gonna have a fucking cracker then what say we burn the fucking place down, eight o'clock in the morning, right after Dean Parrish, we'll torch it, what do you all reckon!?

DANNY Damn right!

MAXINE Eugene . . . calm down.

EUGENE Eugene calm down, ooh me, so sorry . . .

MAXINE Well fuckin' do it, then!

(*Serious eye contact between* EUGENE *and* MAXINE, *like this is on the point of exploding, but it doesn't. A tune comes in, he sits down, disconsolate. Tune fades out.*)

EUGENE I'm . . . I'm frightened.

MAXINE I know you are.

EUGENE It's not all gonna end . . . is it?

(*He looks at her imploringly now, into her eyes. She doesn't know what to say or quite how to respond to him.*)

MAXINE Things . . . end, and then others start don't they, it's . . . I don't know . . . how it is.

EUGENE How it is . . . I don't see why it should have to be.

MAXINE I know you don't.

EUGENE   We'll find somewhere else . . . another all nighter
            . . . different place but same people, same vibe . . .
            after all what's a fucking building? Bricks, plaster,
            who gives a shit about that . . . it's . . . this . . .
            Maxine, us . . . our . . . time.

MAXINE   This . . . it ain't the whole of life.

            (*She sets off out to dance in the precise same spot
            where he watched her dance the first night ever
            he saw her.*)

EUGENE   No . . . but it's the best bit.

            (*Cut to* DANNY *and* SUZANNE.)

SUZANNE   I think you're a really lovely man . . . I have done
            since we spoke in the café that time.

DANNY   Aye . . . well.

SUZANNE   Aye . . . well . . . what?

DANNY   Jesus H Christ, woman!

            (*That's not the response she was hoping for. He
            says no more. The moment lingers, he moves
            away, sits beside* EUGENE. *For a while nothing is
            said.* SUZANNE *looks dejected.*)

EUGENE   Look . . . forget all that other stuff I said . . . I
            don't want us to fall out as well.

DANNY   I'll forget it . . . if you stop being a dickhead and
            even thinking about it.

EUGENE   We're fucked, aren't we?

DANNY   Well and truly.

EUGENE   Gone . . . same way as Geronimo.

DANNY   Oh I don't know . . . didn't he live to a ripe old age
            on the reservation?

EUGENE   My scooter, you cunt . . . not the bloke. Yeah, I
         think he did actually.

DANNY   Crazy Horse got bumped and Sitting Bull died of a
         sore arse . . .

EUGENE   Did he balls, he went of old age as well . . . how
         come you know so much about the native
         Americans, anyway?

DANNY   Well, I've got this mate, and if you tip enough
         gear into him, by about seven in the morning he'll
         blather on more shit about red indians, General
         Custer, the Lone Ranger, Tonto's cousin Barry the
         moccasin mender and every other lost fucking
         cause in history . . .

EUGENE   Is that right?

DANNY   Proper boring get he is!

EUGENE   Is that right?

         (*They are laughing, but gradually reality
         reasserts itself. The two return to silence.*)

EUGENE   I can't go back . . . you know what I mean? But
         what's to go forward to?

DANNY   Life, a wife. The future. Mind you, I think I've
         seen the future.

EUGENE   What, like a vision? Sitting Bull had visions.

DANNY   Aye, well in my one he comes back to life, on a
         scooter, your one . . .

EUGENE   Sitting Bull comes back to life and he's riding
         Geronimo!

DANNY   Like a fucking maniac!

EUGENE   I'm not sure I like that image. The future . . . what
         sort of bollocks is that to be talking? Next you'll
         be telling me my life's in my own hands, it's what I
         make of it.

         (*Both laugh once more.*)

DANNY   It's complete shit all that, isn't it?

EUGENE   Why say it then?

DANNY   I'd hate people to think me negative.

EUGENE   So it's vanity?

DANNY   Yeah. You got any more gear? I'm near through all
         that last lot?

EUGENE   You don't approve of people who sell drugs,
         remember?

DANNY   For a living . . . there's a subtle but important
         difference. Have you?

EUGENE   Yeah . . . My old man thinks I'm just some drug-
         soaked loser . . .

         (EUGENE *slips him the bomb.*)

DANNY   (*sarcastic*) Can't understand that.

EUGENE   He looks at me . . . like I'm . . . weird.

DANNY   So do I.

EUGENE   I'm no loser . . . I've been a winner . . . we're
         winners . . . you and me. It's just . . . we're playing
         a different game to them.

         (DANNY *shapes to pay for the bomb.*)

         Forget about it, on me, selling drugs, sick
         business.

(*Now he sees* Maxine, *and she is looking at him.*)

EUGENE   I just want everything to stay how it is.

DANNY   Aye . . . well. If things stayed the same all the time
          we'd all still be in mud huts, wouldn't we?

          (DANNY *finds his bag/record box, produces a
          single from it.*)

EUGENE   What's that? Sister Lee . . . gold dust.

DANNY   Do you want to buy it?

EUGENE   Buy it?

DANNY   Twenty quid . . . it's yours.

EUGENE   Danny, you'd sell your mother before that record.

DANNY   No I wouldn't . . . but I need the money . . . I'm out
          of my work, my old man's chest is fucked, he can't
          work no more . . .

EUGENE   What else you got in there?

          (DANNY *lifts a stack of records out of his bag, one
          by one they go through them, using the titles as a
          dialogue between them building throughout to a
          climax with 'Tears for Souvenirs'.*)

EUGENE   I Can't Get Away.

DANNY   Better Use Your Head.

EUGENE   What Can I Do?

DANNY   Open the Door to Your Heart.

EUGENE   Breakout.

DANNY   Honest to Goodness.

EUGENE   I wish I had Known.

DANNY   You Got ya Mind on Other Things.

EUGENE   Gotta Get Myself Together.

DANNY   It's an Uphill Climb to the Bottom!

EUGENE   I Can Take Care of Myself.

DANNY   Hit and Run.

EUGENE   Our Love is in the Pocket.

DANNY   One More Hurt.

EUGENE   I Surrender!

DANNY   Too Darn Soulful!

EUGENE   Don't Take it Out on This World!

DANNY   Tears for Souvenirs!

EUGENE   What?

DANNY   Ken Dodd, one of the great unsung northern soul
             heroes.

EUGENE   Right, what are we, the diddy men? Danny, these
             are your . . . your children, you can't sell them!

DANNY   Two hundred and fifty quid the lot, obviously
             Ken's the dearest one . . . pay us when you can.

EUGENE   Man these are . . . oh man . . . here . . .

             (*He commences counting out money, drug money.*)

             I've got hundred . . . I'll get the rest to you when I
             can. Don't worry, you'll get it.

DANNY   I know where you live.

(EUGENE *gives him the cash, takes hold of the
records.* MAXINE *comes over to them.*)

MAXINE   What are you two up to now?

DANNY   A legitimate transaction.

EUGENE   Just bought some records off him.

MAXINE   Smile, Danny . . . it might . . . never . . . alright
         then, it has happened.

DANNY   But smile anyway, you're right.

MAXINE   That's right. You've got to be positive, look to the
         future. You never know what's round the corner.

DANNY   Just what we were saying.

MAXINE   Look to the future, sort your self out Danny, be
         positive . . . it's what I intend to do.

EUGENE   Do you?

DANNY   Floor time!

         (*He bails out to dance.* EUGENE *and* MAXINE *are
         alone, neither quite knows what to say.*)

MAXINE   What's up with you?

EUGENE   Nothing. Nothing's up with me. Except the best
         thing in my . . . in our lives, Maxine, our lives, or
         so I thought, is going and you can spin on a
         fucking sixpence and tell me it ain't no big deal
         and frankly you'll be glad to see the back of it . . .
         how do you think that makes me feel?

MAXINE   How did you think I felt when you quit your job?
         Sold Geronimo . . .

EUGENE   (*quickly*) Not again! We've had that one time and
         again.

MAXINE   I just think we should . . . you should, see it as an opportunity to move on.

EUGENE   I don't want to move on! Why should I have to move on? This has been ace, it's the best thing I've ever known and I don't want to move on. I've . . . been happy, Maxine.

MAXINE   Yes, but . . . There's other stuff, clubs, music, things to do . . .

EUGENE   Other clubs, other music, pop music, punk rock, heavy metal, new romantics, you know what they all are?

MAXINE   Wankers.

EUGENE   To a fucking one! I have no interest in them. I have no interest in jobs. I have no interest in any aspect of this shitty modern world, politics, getting on, getting a job, getting promoted, getting married, getting a better car, suit . . .

MAXINE   Ah well, there you're lying! Getting a better suit you have. No, you might have no interest in all the rest 'cos you don't give a shit about anyone but yourself when it gets down to it! I've never known anyone as utterly vain and selfish as you, truth be told. Cars, jobs, houses might be shit but Eugene has to be the best turned out speed freak in town.

EUGENE   Some things count, I agree.

MAXINE   You see . . . I think I have.

EUGENE   Have what?

MAXINE   Interest in other stuff.

EUGENE   I know well you have . . . I know it . . . I can see it . . . in you!

MAXINE   So?

EUGENE   So? So . . . what is it Maxine? What is it . . . that
          turns you on? If it's not . . . being with me?

MAXINE   When did I say that? Eugene, being with you . . .
          used to be the one and only thing in the world
          that I thought about.

EUGENE   Did it.

MAXINE   Yeah . . . but . . .

EUGENE   But what?

MAXINE   ˙You've . . . changed . . . 'cos of the gear, and . . .

EUGENE   Oh, the fucking gear, Geronimo wah wah wah . . .
          Welcome to the last night of Wigan Casino! . . . I
          wonder if the last hours on the Titanic were this
          much fun.

MAXINE   I reckon you're the one bloke could have made 'em
          even worse. Oh why can't things stay the same,
          simple?

EUGENE   You just said you wanted to move on.

MAXINE   Well.

EUGENE   Ah . . . see . . . caught you out.

MAXINE   Too clever by half . . . I mean move on in a . . . a . . .
          stay the same sort of way.

EUGENE   That makes sense. Maxine, some days stood by
          that meat counter I could have broke down and
          cried . . . I'm sorry if you loved it back then but I . . .
          no way . . . no fucking way missis . . . I'm off
          through to M's.

          (*He gets up and leaves, but does not disappear
          entirely. Alone, she ponders.* SUZANNE *comes up.*)

MAXINE   Suzanne if you say one more thing about dying
          I'm gonna knock you out.

SUZANNE   Oh . . . alright then I won't. (*Heavy sarcastic.*) But
             face it Maxine, we're all going to!

MAXINE   Get lost!

SUZANNE   One day or another! We'll all die!

MAXINE   I know . . . and guess what!

SUZANNE   What?

MAXINE   This for you is that day!

SUZANNE   No please, my mum'll be furious with you.

MAXINE   Will she? And Graham in Burnley, I couldn't deny
             him his happiness . . . the poor swine . . . man will
             he regret at his own leisure.

SUZANNE   Don't say that!

MAXINE   Sorry . . . gosh, raw nerve. I know he won't, he'll
             spend his life laughing at how round the bend you
             are . . .

SUZANNE   He won't.

MAXINE   He will, he'll call you 't' wife', or 'ar lass', and if
             you say it, insist upon it, one way or the other
             he'll end up doing it and he'll be glad to 'cos it'll
             make you happy . . .

SUZANNE   He won't.

MAXINE   Course he will, be a mug if he didn't. Don't know
             how lucky he is, though I reckon he does deep
             down, what must he think about you coming here
             every Saturday?

SUZANNE   He don't think owt . . .

MAXINE   Does he never say anything about it?

SUZANNE   No . . . 'cos he don't exist.

MAXINE   He must wonder what you get up to I mean not
           getting home till Sunday dinnertime . . . He what?

           (SUZANNE'S *face says it all. Sadly, unbeknownst to
           her,* EUGENE *has remained within earshot of the
           following.*)

SUZANNE   I made him up . . . why do you think you've never
           seen him?

MAXINE   'Cos . . . you've? I just thought 'cos he wouldn't
           like it here so you've never brought him . . . he
           don't exist . . . at all?

SUZANNE   There's a lad in Burnley, and he's called Graham
           . . . and I went out with him . . . about three times
           about three years ago . . . but he never asked me
           again.

MAXINE   Well . . . why've you . . . ?

SUZANNE   Because you met Eugene here and he loves you so
           much and . . . I just felt . . . really shit . . . and I
           started saying there was this guy at home who
           likes me . . . and I liked the idea of it, but . . . he
           doesn't. When I see him about half the time he
           don't even let on.

MAXINE   Oh, Suzanne . . . come here.

SUZANNE   I couldn't . . . go away having lied to you all along
           . . . I'm scared I won't see you again after tonight.

           (*The girls hug.* EUGENE *steps forward into their
           light.*)

EUGENE   Well fuck my old boots, I've heard the best of it
           now!

           (MAXINE *rounds on him instantly.*)

MAXINE   You shurrup and get lost! You weren't supposed
            to be listening!

EUGENE   You *are* called Suzanne? I mean the dry cleaners,
            that's not shit as well, is it?

MAXINE   I'm warning you!

EUGENE   Jesus, she could be anyone!

MAXINE   And she still wouldn't be a twat like you, now bog
            off into M's and leave us alone.

            (EUGENE *makes his way away from them shaking
            his head and laughing.*)

SUZANNE   Don't be mad with him . . . let's face it he's
            laughing 'cos it's funny . . .

MAXINE   And 'cos he can laugh at everyone else, but if
            anyone laughed at him he'd start frothin' at the
            mouth. Suzanne . . . this is true now, in't it . . . not
            another wind up?

            (SUZANNE'S *face tells her it is clearly, sadly, true.*)

MAXINE   Oh, well . . . you shouldn't . . . (*Stops, searches for
            the words.*)

SUZANNE   I shouldn't what?

MAXINE   Feel like that . . . Have to feel like that, you've . . .

SUZANNE   Maxine, if you're gonna tell me I'm beautiful and
            there's loads of lads who'd be desperate to go out
            with me if only they met me, don't, because . . .

MAXINE   It's not true, I know.

SUZANNE   Cheers.

MAXINE   There'll be some . . . a few . . . one . . .

SUZANNE   Madman.

MAXINE   Somewhere.

SUZANNE   Well where the hell is he then!?

MAXINE   I think I got him before you.

SUZANNE   No you didn't. I'm scared my life'll just be work, sleep, watch telly wi' my mum and dad . . . and get old.

MAXINE   Don't be daft, why's it have to be that?

SUZANNE   You've got . . . the first time I ever saw you three quarters of the lads on the dance floor had their eye on you . . . and you can say it's not important and why should it matter and it's what's inside but that's all bollocks, really.

MAXINE   No, it's . . . it's . . . you're right it's bollocks, it's got a lot to do with what you look like.

SUZANNE   Exactly. If they all want into your knickers it's worth a lot of being a nice girl.

MAXINE   You are a really nice girl though.

            (SUZANNE *is on the point of breaking down utterly.*)

            No, it is about being a nice person.

SUZANNE   It isn't.

MAXINE   It is.

SUZANNE   It isn't.

MAXINE   Oh, but it is.

SUZANNE   Is it shit! I can't suck being a nice girl till it comes all over me, can I!?

MAXINE   Well, no, you can't do that.

SUZANNE   Well then. Being a nice girl an't got me anywhere,
           Maxine!

MAXINE   Point taken . . . if you get my meaning.

SUZANNE   Oh I do.

MAXINE   You are so bad! What a thing to say!

SUZANNE   It's true!

MAXINE   When I first met you you'd never have said
           anything like that!

           (MAXINE, *once again, is laughing her socks off at*
           SUZANNE.)

MAXINE   I am gonna miss you so much . . . oh shit . . . oh
           my God, I'm gonna go fucking mad tonight!

SUZANNE   What's matter?

MAXINE   (*very sad*) Eugene. I love him . . . but he . . . he
           wears me out . . . it never ends with him, he's
           wizzing off his nuts . . . in fact, it goes back to
           what we were just talking about, guess when
           were't last time he shagged me?

SUZANNE   Half past eight before you came out?

MAXINE   I wish . . . it must be three months since.

SUZANNE   Three months!? Is he off his head?

MAXINE   I've just said that . . . he's that far gone it's just
           for weeing with . . . when he can find it.

           (SUZANNE *gives her a very strange and curious*
           look.)

MAXINE   The wizz . . . it does that to lads.

SUZANNE   What?

MAXINE   It . . . shrinks it . . . and they stop wanting to shag
           you all the time.

SUZANNE   It never does? God, if I lived with my boyfriend
           . . . There'd be none of that . . . I'd have him
           through his paces morning noon and night, he'd
           have no energy for nighters, believe you me.

MAXINE   Well . . . that's what you think . . . but it in't like
           that . . . once you've been shacked up a few month
           . . . he starts turning onto his side and pretending
           to be asleep. Or he stays up till three in't morning
           after you've gone to bed so he can be on his own
           and he knows you'll be asleep when he climbs in.
           Or he shags you 'cos he thinks he ought to and
           you know full well his eyes are shut 'cos he's
           thinking about lesbo's a go-go in Men Only or
           somat. And there's not a lot you can do.

SUZANNE   Kinky underwear?

MAXINE   Looks better in pictures than real life.

SUZANNE   Oh . . . you've tried it then?

MAXINE   . . . To a degree.

SUZANNE   . . . Right . . . what degree?

MAXINE   None of your business. Oh, I'm sorry I've
           depressed you with my stuff when you've got
           more than enough to be down about already.

SUZANNE   You're going to go to university and be an high
           flyer, aren't you?

MAXINE   Where did that come from?

SUZANNE   I can see it . . . you're cut out for it . . . there's
           loads of stuff you could do, you should go and do
           it, all of it. Let him stew on his own if he wants.

MAXINE   I think I've cocked my life up sometimes.

SUZANNE   You haven't . . . that's just how it feels . . . but
           from where I'm sat you haven't.

           (*The first of the 'three before 8.00' tunes comes
           in. The girls look at one another, then they hug.
           Cut to* DANNY *as* EUGENE *enters and comes
           straight up to him.*)

EUGENE   Danny . . . all these years I've known you . . . you
           have been a maintenance man at the engineering
           works, haven't you? I mean it's not . . . all
           bollocks, is it?

DANNY   No, why?

EUGENE   Oh thank fuck for that, world's fuckin' moving on
           me tonight man I tell you, I can't keep with this . . .

DANNY   It's the gear man, I keep tellin you.

EUGENE   Will you fuck off with that one as well, what's the
           matter with everyone round here?

DANNY   Suit yourself . . . not long now.

EUGENE   Till when?

DANNY   Dawn.

           (EUGENE *looks at him a moment.*)

EUGENE   Well it's not like they're gonna shoot us or owt,
           don't say it like that.

           (*They pause and reflect.*)

DANNY   I've always hated these three records . . . the
           'three before 8.00'. Every week, when I hear Toby
           Legend kick in . . . it's like a fucking sentence for
           me.

EUGENE   Well, look on the bright side . . . you won't hear
           'em again, will you?

DANNY   No. I won't.

EUGENE   Course you will, there'll be other nights.

DANNY   Not for me.

EUGENE   What you talking about?

DANNY   That's it for me, man.

EUGENE   What?

DANNY   The scene . . . nighters . . . (*Shakes his head.*)
            gone. Time to change the picture . . . there'll never
            be fuck all like this again . . . I'm not gonna try.

EUGENE   Don't . . . please . . . don't say that.

DANNY   I'm not trekking round the country looking for
            something that's gone.

EUGENE   Don't say that . . .

DANNY   Alright, I won't say it if makes you feel better,
            but . . .

EUGENE   Oh, why's it . . . why's it had to come to this!? I
            thought you'd always . . . no matter what you'd be
            staying the course, keep the faith man! What does
            it mean!? Keep the fucking faith! Why do you
            think we've all said it all these years . . . don't
            duck out on me now, man! When I need you the
            most . . .

DANNY   Look . . . can't you see it? Wigan Casino . . .
            closing . . . my engineering works . . . closing . . .
            things . . . closing . . . these times . . . they've
            come to a close, man.

EUGENE   So . . . what? We all sit down and fucking die?

DANNY   Get with it . . . or be trampled under it I reckon. I'm
            gonna go find Suzanne, say bye bye to her . . .

(*He walks away.* EUGENE *stands up after he has
gone.*)

EUGENE   No! . . . (*Imploringly, pathetically, weakly.*)
            Danny . . . ?

            (DANNY *turns to face him, then slowly shakes his
            head.* EUGENE *looks like a little boy whose mum
            just walked out on him, again. He looks round,*
            MAXINE *is there.*)

MAXINE   You are a just a total wanker . . . do you know
            that?

            (*He takes it stoically, mellow even, nods, gives
            her a thumbs up.*)

EUGENE   Cheers. I've always suspected it but confirmation
            is good. I had no idea how shit my company
            actually was until this evening.

MAXINE   Stop feeling so bleeding sorry for yourself.

EUGENE   I've got a lot to feel sorry about . . . my club's
            shutting . . . I can't get on with you no more . . .
            people I care about are . . . giving up on it all . . .
            moving on . . . I'm unemployed when it comes
            down to it and pretty well unemployable.

MAXINE   And you've got the social skills of a . . .

            (*She can't find the words.*)

EUGENE   Of a . . . ? (*He helps her out with a few
            suggestions.*) A blocked drain . . . a backed-up
            toilet . . . an Irishman?

MAXINE   Why do you always have to go on about Irishmen
            as well?

EUGENE   'Cos I've spent all my life wi' one and if they're all
            like him . . .

MAXINE   Do you know how much you talk about him?

EUGENE   Sorry, do I get boring?

MAXINE   No . . . you never get boring. I just don't know
            why you can't just accept him for how he is. He
            were always a sweetheart when I met him.

EUGENE   That's 'cos you're female . . . and offered him
            serious hope that he might never see me again. Ah
            well . . . time to change . . . grow up . . . get serious
            . . . straighten out. Join the working men's club
            and play doms with him on Sundays . . .

            (*There is silence between them a few moments, as
            the music comes back in.*)

MAXINE   Eugene . . . what you said . . . it's true, isn't it?
            We . . . don't get on any more. Do we?

            (*He doesn't say anything, looks sad, she comes to
            him, sits with him, puts her head on his shoulder.
            The last of the 'three before 8.00', Dean Parrish,
            begins to play.*)

EUGENE   Oh shit . . . don't cry. (*Pause.*)

MAXINE   Not long now . . . I'm frightened.

EUGENE   Me too, pet . . . stay here a minute. I aren't telling
            you I'm . . . any good, Maxine . . . but I've loved
            you, and I've loved northern soul . . . and I've
            loved Wigan Casino . . . and I don't think that's
            bad. You do . . . what you've got to do.

MAXINE   These times . . . here, with you . . . listening to you
            argue the toss about 60s, 70s, crossover . . . which
            one's a northern tune and which is just shitty pop
            music . . .

EUGENE   Important stuff.

MAXINE   Crucial stuff . . . I don't want them to be over,
            Eugene.

EUGENE   Me neither . . . but they are.

MAXINE   I wish you could get another scooter . . .

EUGENE   Chair.

MAXINE   Sorry, and we could go out on it like we used to.

EUGENE   Angel, you know I could never replace Geronimo.

MAXINE   No.

EUGENE   I'll never love anyone else, Maxine.

MAXINE   You will.

EUGENE   I won't. I'm five minutes away from nothing . . .
            Blokes have walked to the gas chambers happier
            than I'll walk out of here when it's shut . . .

MAXINE   I'll always be your friend . . .

EUGENE   No . . . you'll never be just that . . . every time I
            see you it'll be like a knife straight through me . . .
            and I don't mind you knowing . . .

            (*They hug one another, in what is their last few
            moments. Across the stage* DANNY *finds* SUZANNE.)

DANNY   Look, you take care, good luck, be sure and marry
            that man in Burnley, Gary, Graham, whoever he
            is . . .

            (*She doesn't quite know what to say.*)

            Aye aye . . . well . . . take care . . .

            (*He gives her a kiss and a hug. Turns to go.*)

SUZANNE   Danny . . . will I see you again?

DANNY   I'm . . . probably not.

SUZANNE   I always thought . . . one day . . . we might . . . you
            know . . .

DANNY   Aye . . . well . . . I couldn't deal with some brick
            shithouse from Burnley after me with a pick axe
            handle, could I? Wouldn't blame him, either . . .
            he's a lucky man. A very lucky man. Take care.

SUZANNE   . . . And you . . . bye.

            (DANNY *departs to his bag and to get his stuff.*
            Dean Parrish ends, the house lights go on, and it
            is like dawn has risen, daylight streaming in from
            all portholes as it were. There are a few moments
            of silence between them all, rubbing their eyes,
            etc. DANNY *looks in his bag, and takes out his*
            records, looks at them in surprise. EUGENE *has*
            put them back. He looks at EUGENE.)

EUGENE   Their yours. Keep 'em.

DANNY   What about the money?

EUGENE   (*quickly*) Forget about it . . . keep the faith, man.

            (*Frank Wilson's, 'Do I Love You' plays. All have*
            their last dance as the lights fade down on the
            stage. After this the actors take their bow, as the
            screens slowly fade to the images of the destroyed
            Casino, devastated by fire, etc.)

            As the audience gets up to leave the following
            text appears on screen:

            'Wigan Casino closed down in November 1981,
            shortly afterwards it was devastated by fire. The
            proposed new Town Hall for Wigan was never
            built, and the Casino site at Station Road is now a
            car park.'

PS: Suzanne met a man called Terry in 1982 and
        married him the following year. She shares him to
        this day with a sofa and Burnley Football Club

        Danny returned to his native north east and in
        1983 met a woman called Janice and fathered two
        children. Alas, they got divorced in 1996 and
        shortly after he attended his first all nighter in 15
        years. He is currently making up for lost time . . .

        Maxine attended Manchester Polytechnic where
        she studied Criminology. She has a BSC, an MA, a
        PhD, a driving licence and all things else. She is
        the author of numerous books on all manner of
        sociological subject. She has never married.

        Eugene returned to his native Bolton and joined
        the working men's club with his dad, who sadly
        died in 1996. He never did replace Geronimo. He is
        presently captain of the darts and dominoes team
        and runs the weekly northern nights in the Good
        Room. He has never married and lives alone in the
        house he was brought up in.

        Wigan Casino – gone but not forgotten. To all
        who loved and lived it: KEEP THE FAITH!

        Special thanks and all respect be to Russ
        Winstanley, the founder of the Casino.